The Pied Poets

The Pied Poets

CONTEMPORARY VERSE OF THE
TRANSYLVANIAN AND DANUBE
GERMANS OF
ROMANIA

FOREST
BOOKS
London & Boston

Selected &
Translated
by

Robert Elsie

PUBLISHED BY
FOREST BOOKS

20 Forest View, Chingford, London E4 7AY, U.K.
16 Lincoln Road, Wayland, MA 01778, U.S.A.

First published 1990

Typeset in Great Britain by Cover to Cover, Cambridge
Printed in Great Britain by BPCC Wheatons Ltd, Exeter

British Library Cataloguing in Publication Data:

The Pied Poets: contemporary verse of the Transylvanian
& Danube Germans of Romania.
1. Poetry in German, 1945. Anthologies. English texts
831'91408

ISBN 0–948259–77–9

Library of Congress Catalogue Card No.

89–85285

Contents

INTRODUCTION by Robert Elsie   viii

OSKAR PASTIOR
The shiver poem   3
If the street sweepers in Reschinar   5
Of all the epistemological affairs   7
In the first line   9

NIKOLAUS BERWANGER
Im memoriam L.   13
Advertisement   15
Dry eyes   17
Snow White open your eyes   20
Images of an absurd June   23
Honestly   25
Late joy   25

CLAUS STEPHANI
Marmatia   29
Biography   31
Pompeii, Via Stabiana   33
Poetry Club   35
Fortified church in Transylvania   37

ANEMONE LATZINA
In the morning   41
13 July 1974   43
Lament for all I've lost to this wide world   45
In July 1977   47

FRIEDER SCHULLER
Indian summer in a department store   51
Perhaps I'd take my coffee mug   53

Franz Hodjak

Scope   57
Reiner Kunze   59
At the cemetery   61
Advice   63
Ovid in exile   65
Upon reading poems by Weinheber in view of   67
     his success in the Thirties
Transcending borders   67
Villon's arrival in heaven   70
Autobiography   73
Savonarola   75
Daily routine   77

Rolf Frieder Marmont

Spacious seconds   81
Dobruja realm of shade   83
Children   85

Johann Lippet

Onetime spate of suicides in the family   90
My neighbour makes a poem for me   93
Weekend. The head   95
Also. An Arts Poetica   97
Every evening   99

Werner Söllner

Life. An example   103
Right through this house   105
Departure   107
Wall, nail, picture   107

William Totok

Workers at the brickyard   111
Anna Espresso, Váci St., Budapest, 27 July 1979   113
Departure   115
Seasons   117
Normal day   119
The flag   119

Rolf Bossert

Short poem on a little freezing bird   123

Artists, critics & cabbage salad 125
Golden age of fables 127
About my life 129
Season 131
Nightshade rift 133
Confidence 133

RICHARD WAGNER
Dialectics 137
Words of the poet 139
The waitress 141
Question for Mandel'shtam 143
Song 145
With the painter Lauterbach 147
The burning table (from a postcard) 147
I was a statue 149

ERNEST WICHNER
Slogan 153
Trakl in exile 155

HORST SAMSON
Trip to Paris 159
Morning 161
Punctual curriculum vitae 163
Snow poem for Edda 165
Meeting of poets in Sighişoara 167
    'Vlad Dracul' Restaurant
Isolation 169
Holidays at home 171
Winter morning 173
Winter poem for Sarah Kirsch 175
Federico 177
Subsequent remark about my birth 179

CARMEN PUCHIANU
Postcard for Frank O'Hara 183
Timeless 183

JULIANA MODOI
Village evening 187
A mother's consolation 187

Introduction

The Pied Poets is both an anthology of the most recent poetic activity of the German-speaking minority from the Transylvanian and Danube (Banat) regions of Romania and a commemorative monument, a somewhat frivolous poetic tombstone if you will, marking the passing of a literature and culture. This volume does not set out to be a comprehensive anthology of German-Romanian literature, but an introduction for the English speaking reader to the so-called 'fifth German literature'a (after that of West Germany, East Germany, Austria and Switzerland) which has come to an end after five centuries of existence.

The German population of Romania, which still constitutes the second largest national minority in that country (after the 1,700,000 Hungarians), comprises two traditionally distinct groups: the Transylvanian Saxons (Siebenbürger Sachsen) in the centre of the country and the Danube or Banat Swabians (Donauschwaben or Banater Schwaben) on the western border with Yugoslavia.

The German minority of Transylvania are the descendents of colonists invited to settle there in 1150AD by the Hungarian King Geza II 'to defend the crown'. Although called Saxons, from a linguistic point of view they are of Moselle Franconian origin, stemming not from Saxony but principally from the Moselle, northern Lorraine, Luxembourg and Flanders. In Transylvania they founded a number of cities and about 250 smaller settlements, and in 1224 were granted special privileges under the 'Privilegium Andreanum' of King Andrew II. The Lutheran reform movement introduced by Johannes Honterus was widely followed in Transylvania, and in their fortified churches (Kirchenburgen), the 'Saxons', albeit more than once impoverished and decimated by marauding hoards, managed to withstand both the Ottoman Turks spreading Islam and the Viennese bent on imposing the Counter-Reformation, and to maintain their bastion of German Protestant culture over the centuries. In 1940, there were still 250,000 German speakers in Transylvania, though evacuation, deportation and emigration during and after the Second World War have now reduced their numbers to well under 150,000.

The Danube or Banat Swabians settled in the eighteenth century in Banat, the frontier region (formerly governed by a 'ban') between Hungary, Yugoslavia and Romania. They originated primarily from southwestern Germany as the name Swabian indicates. Their first settlements were established in 1722–1726 under Emperor Charles VI of Austria, followed by waves of emigration under Maria Theresa in 1763–1770 and under Joseph II in 1782–1787 to repopulate Habsburg territories devasted by war and epidemics. The Treaty of Trianon in 1919 divided the region among Yugoslavia, Romania and Hungary. The population of Banat nevertheless remained very mixed with a distinct German element. Of the three countries, it is only in Romania that a substantial German-speaking minority still exists. In 1939 there were 450,000 Danube Swabians. They now number less than 150,000. Prominent among the Danube Swabians are the German 'Weltschmerz' poet Nikolaus Lenau (1802–1850) born in Csatád (Lenauheim) and Tarzan himself, Johnny Weissmuller, whose family came from Freidorf.

Romania was the only country in Eastern Europe not to expel its German minority after the Second World War. The Germans there are now recognized as an official national minority (or cohabiting nation), and benefit at least from the same rights as the Romanians themselves. During the 1980s, however, when the Ceauşescu dictatorship was driving the country into a state of political and cultural isolation and economic ruin, emigration of the two groups to West Germany increased dramatically. By the end of the 1980s, almost all Germans living in Romania desperately longed to leave the country which had become a living nightmare of fear and repression, but very few were allowed to do so. Many of those who were able to emigrate were bought out discreetly by the West German government at up to DM 11,000 per person. Germans and Jews were cynically referred to as Romania's top export articles, and not without reason perhaps. Though many of the older people understandably chose to stay put, the steady drain on the younger population, coupled with inevitable assimilation, whether natural or actively encouraged by the authorities in Bucharest, brought about stagnation in virtually all spheres of German cultural life in Romania. With over fifty percent of German-Romanians now living in the West, the Christmas 1989 revolution and political opening up of the country after so many years of darkness will no doubt result in a further rapid increase in emigration.

The effects of the period of stagnation have been particularly dramatic on German literature which in Romania enjoys a tradition going back many centuries. Ernest Wichner states unequivocally in his preface to a recent anthology of poetry and prose that the end is in sight.

> 'The generation of authors now in their thirties and forties constitute the last German writers in Romania. It is becoming obvious that their numbers have fallen below the critical mass essential for the cultural survival of the German minority there. As opposed to the early seventies, when a dozen or so young authors all began publishing at the same time, there is hardly a young German-language author left with enough linguistic competence to be worthy of support.'[1]

The impact of German-Romanian literature in the twentieth century has not been entirely marginal, despite its peripheral situation. Indeed, twentieth-century German literature as a whole has to a good extent been the creation of fringe groups in political, social or geographical isolation from the mainstream. Paul Celan (1920–1970) born in Czernowitz, for instance, is among the leading German poets of the twentieth century. The integration of the many other Jewish writers into the German mainstream was always ambiguous, most of them living, nolens volens, in some sort of periphery. During the Nazi dictatorship of the thirties and forties, most other German writers of talent found themselves in exile, whether external or internal. Changing borders and the post-war division of Germany

---

[1]'Das Wohnen ist kein Ort. Texte und Zeichen aus Siebenbürgen, dem Banat und den Gegenden versuchter Ankunft'. Die Horen, Zeitschrift für Literatur, Kunst und Kritik 147 (Hanover 1987), p.5.

and Europe forced many writers to reassess their attitudes to the powers that be and many found themselves in the wrong spot. It is this forced introspection and an awareness of one's difference which have often contributed to the outbursts of creativity which German letters, especially in Romania, have always enjoyed.

The last twenty-five years are generally regarded as the zenith of German poetry in Romania, culminating a long tradition. The origins of German literature there lie in the High Middle Ages. Among 15th century works of note are the memoirs of Helene Kottaner of Braşov (Kronstadt) and the anonymous 'Türkenbüchlein'. Johannes Honterus (1498–1549), the reformer, introduced Lutheran German as a literary language in Transylvania and set up a printing press, the first one in southeastern Europe. The 17th century was the age of Protestant hymnists and pietist poets, among whom was J. Kelp (Kelpius) (1673–1708) who emigrated to Pennsylvania. The Romantic movement of 19th century Europe made its impact felt in Transylvania and Banat, too. The Banat newspaper 'Temeswarer Zeitung' (Timişoara Newspaper), founded in 1852, served as an important vehicle of communication for the German minority until 1949. German-Romanian folk songs and folklore material were collected and printed by numerous writers and scholars. Poetry of all genres, both in standard German and in 'Saxon' and 'Swabian' dialects, was produced and published, together with short stories, novels and plays. Adam Müller-Guttenbrunn (1852–1923) portrayed the romantic pathos of village life among the Danube Germans in his classic 19th century novels. But it was Adolf Meschendörfer's journal 'Die Karpathen' (The Carpathians) published from 1907 to 1914 which first paved the way to a more cosmopolitan literature, in Transylvania in particular. Both German communities also began to show interest in their Hungarian and Romanian neighbours and the veil of provinciality receded.

The Klingsor Circle named after the literary periodical Klingsor published between 1924 and 1939 was associated with the works of Karl Bernhard Capesius, Heinrich Zillich and Erwin Wittstock. Nowadays one can no longer speak of two separate German literatures in Romania. Since 1945, the literary traditions of the Transylvanian and Danube Germans have merged and their intellectual centre is no longer Braşov (Kronstadt), Cluj-Napoca (Klausenburg) or Timişoara (Temeswar), but Bucharest where the literary magazine 'Neue Literatur' (New Literature) has been published since 1956. Among the classical authors of 20th century German poetry in Romania are Oscar Walter Cisek (1898–1966), Alfred Margul-Sperber (1898–1967) and Wolf von Aichelburg (1912—).

Though one must not forget that Transylvania is geographically closer to the Crimea, to Istanbul and Asia than it is to Berlin and Munich, German-Romanian literature has always been an essentially Central European literature. Many a dour Lutheran pastor in the fortified churches at the foot of the Carpathians would indeed have shuddered at the thought of being in the heart of the Balkans. This dichotomy (some would call it collective schizophrenia) has often been more a source of disorientation than a blessing.

Has there ever really been a German Romania? Ernest Wichner thinks not. The ancestors of the German Romanians once set off with pioneer fervour to 'go east, young man' in order to found a better Germany. The road was beset with the stumbling blocks of history, politics and economics. Now the present generation is returning to its origins, some with the naive expectation of bringing back a better Romania with them. What awaits them in West Germany, the promised land, is no more than reintegration into the mainstream from which they originally fled. German Romania, if it ever did really exist, may now rest in peace.

Be this as it may, it would be misleading to envisage German-Romanian literature as brooding nostalgically on the problems of exile or preoccupied with socio-political issues and the loss of its quaint folklore traditions. Its contemporary verse, almost disappointingly bereft of local colour, mirrors a whole gamut of familiar human emotions and intellectual pursuits, and is surprisingly in tune with the Western world. It is to be hoped that in this volume, the English-speaking reader may recognize and enjoy these subtle, remote and yet hardly alien reflections of a vanishing world.

It remains simply for me to thank all those who have assisted me in one way or another in the completion of this project, among whom: Inter Nationes (Bonn) and the Arts Council of Great Britain for their generous publication grants, Elisabeth Ernst of the West German Embassy in Bucharest, Richard Wagner (Berlin) and Barbara Schultz (Ottawa).

Robert Elsie
Olzheim/Eifel

Linguist, translator and critic, Robert Elsie was born in Vancouver, Canada, in 1950. He studied at the University of British Columbia, the Free University of Berlin, the Ecole Pratique des Hautes Etudes in Paris and the Dublin Institute for Advanced Studies, finishing his doctorate in Celtic Studies at the University of Bonn in 1978. In addition to numerous translations, he is the author of *Dictionary of Albanian Literature* (New York, 1986) and *Dialect Relationships in Goidelic* (Hamburg, 1986).

Acknowledgements

Forest Books gratefully acknowledge financial support for this publication from the Arts Council of Great Britain and from Inter Nationes, Bonn.

We gratefully acknowledge the following sources:

OSKAR PASTIOR: *Das Fröstelgedicht, In der ersten Zeile:* Gedichtgedichte (Luchterhand, Darmstadt 1973), *Wenn in Reschinar, Von all den Erkenntnisgeschäften:* Höricht (Klaus Ramm, Spenge 1975). NIKOLAUS BERWANGER: *In Memoriam L., Werbetext, Trockene Augen:* Spätes Bekenntnis (Kriterion, Bucharest 1979), *Schneewittchen öffne deine Augen, Späte Freude:* Schneewittchen öffne deine Augen (Facla, Timişoara 1980), *Ehrlich, Absurde Junibilder:* An meine ungeborene Enkel (Facla, Timişoara 1983). CLAUS STEPHANI: *Siebenbürgische Kirchenburg, Marmatien, Biographie:* Ruf ins offene Land (Kriterion, Bucharest 1980), *Pompei, Via Stabiana, Poesie Club:* Draußen singt Dorkia (Kriterion, Bucharest 1985). ANEMONE LATZINA: *Am Morgen:* Was man heute so dichten kann (Kriterion, Bucharest 1971), *13. Juli 1974, Im Juli 1977, Klagefragen nach allem was ich an diese weite Welt verloren:* Neue Literatur (Bucharest). FRIEDER SCHULLER: *Vielleicht meine Kaffeeschale:* Paß nach Transsylvanien (Urheber Verlag, Bonn 1979). *Altweibersommer im Kaufhaus:* Einladung zu einer Schüssel Palukes (Parnaß, Bonn 1980. FRANZ HODJAK: *Spielräume, Reiner Kunze:* Spielräume (Kriterion, Bucharest 1974), *Im Friedhof, Ratschlag, Alltag, Ovid im Exil, Nach der Lektüre von Gedichten Weinhebers im Rückblick auf seinen Erfolg in den Dreissigerjahren:* Offene Briefe (Kriterion, Bucharest 1976), *Villons Ankunft im Himmel:* Mit Polly Knall spricht man über selbstverständliche Dinge als wären sie selbstverständlich (Kriterion, Bucharest 1979), *Über alle Grenzen hinweg, Autobiographie, Savonarola:* Flieder im Ohr (Kriterion, Bucharest 1983). ROLF FRIEDER MARMONT: *Kinder, Geräumige Sekunden:* Fünfte Jahreszeit (Dacia, Cluj-Napoca 1974), *Schattenreich Dobrudscha:* Lichtkaskaden (Kriterion, Bucharest 1984). JOHANN LIPPET: *Jeden Abend:* Wortmeldungen, eine Anthologie junger Lyriker aus dem Banat (Facla, Timişoara 1972), *Gewesener Selbstmordgang der Familie:* Vorläufige Protokolle, Anthologie junger rumäniendeutscher Lyrik (Dacia, Cluj-Napoca 1976), *Mein Nachbar macht mir ein Gedicht, Wochenende. Der Kopf, Auch. Eine Ars Poetica:* So wars im Mai so ist es (Kriterion, Bucharest 1984). WERNER SÖLLNER: *Abschied:* Mitteilungen eines Privatmannes (Dacia, Cluj-Napoca 1978), *Leben, Ein Beispiel:* Eine Entwöhnung (Kriterion, Bucharest 1980), *Quer durch dies Haus:* Kopfland. Passagen (Suhrkamp, Frankfurt 1988), *Mauer, Nagel, Bild:* manuscript. WILLIAM TOTOK: *Arbeiter in der Ziegelei:* Vergesellschaftung der Gefühle (Kriterion, Bucharest 1984), *Anna Espresso, Váci-Utca, Budapest, den 27. Juli 1979, Gewöhnlicher Tag, Jahreszeiten:* Freundliche Fremdheit (Facla, Timişoara 1980), *Die Fahne:* manuscript. ROLF BOSSERT: *Das kurze Gedicht vom kleinen frierenden Vogel, Künstler Kritiker & Krautsalat:* Befragung Heute (Kriterion, Bucharest 1974), *Aus meinem Leben, Goldne Zeiten der Fabel:* Siebensachen (Kriterion, Bucharest 1979), *Jahreszeit:* Neuntöter (Dacia, Cluj-Napoca 1984), *Zuversicht:* Neue Literatur, *Nachtschattenriß:* manuscript. RICHARD WAGNER: *Dialektik, Dichterworte:* Invasion der Uhren (Kriterion, Bucharest 1977), *Ich war ein Denkmal:* Klartext (Albatros, Bucharest 1973), *Die Kellnerin:* Hotel California 1 (Kriterion, Bucharest 1980), *Frage an Mandelstam:* Hotel California 2 (Kriterion, Bucharest 1981), *Lied:* Das Auge des Feuilletons, Geschichten und Notizen, (Dacia, Cluj-Napoca 1984), *Mit dem Maler Lauterbach, Der brennende Tisch (nach einer Postkarte):* manuscript. ERNEST WICHNER: *Trakl im Exil, Losung:* Steinsuppe (Suhrkamp, Frankfurt 1988). HORST SAMSON: *Reise nach Paris, Pünktlicher Lebenslauf, Schneegedicht für Edda:* Reiberfläche (Kriterion, Bucharest 1982), *Morgen:* Tiefflug (Dacia, Cluj-Napoca 1981), *Schässburger Dichtertreffen, Verinselung, Urlaub im Zimmer, Wintermorgen, Wintergedicht für Sarah Kirsch, Federico, Nachbemerkung zu meiner Geburt:* Lebraum (Dacia, Cluj-Napoca 1985). JULIANA MODOI: *Dorfabend, Der Trost einer Mutter:* Der Zweite Horizont (Dacia, Cluj 1988). CARMEN PUCHIANU: *Postkarte an Frank O'Hara, Zeitlos:* Der Zweite Horizont (Dacia, Cluj 1988).

Oskar Pastior

(1927–)

Pastior was born in 1927 in Sibiu (Hermannstadt) in Transylvania where he attended school until 1944. After five years of deportation in the Ukraine following the end of World War II, he returned in 1949 to his native city. He began studies of German language and literature in Bucharest in 1955 and worked from 1960 to 1968 as an editor for the German-language services of the Romanian radio network. In 1968 he emigrated via Austria to West Berlin where he presently lives. Pastior's playful poetics have given him a reputation as one of the few contemporary German writers with a genuine sense of humour. He has published over seventeen volumes of verse and translations (Tristan Tzara, Francesco Petrarch, Viktor Khlebnikov and Urmuz), plus plays for radio and 'acoustic poetry'.

Das fröstelgedicht fröstelt bei der vorstellung es bestünde aus einem sprachvorgang der behaupten könne es habe sich in ihm ein denkvorgang dermaßen verselbständigt daß er in seinem sprachvorgang bei der vorstellung zu frösteln fröstele das fröstelgedicht ist töricht daß es so was denkt denn wie kann man schon bei der vorstellung zu frösteln frösteln.

The shiver poem shivers at the thought that it consists of a linguistic process capable of affirming that a thought process consolidated itself in it to such an extent that in its linguistic process the shiver poem shivers at the thought of shivering the shiver poem is silly to think so because how can you shiver at the thought of shivering

Wenn in Reschinar die Straßenkehrer entweder zwei rechte oder zwei linke Beine haben, so liegt Reschinar sehr abseits von anderen Gebirgsdörfern. Der Schwung ihres Besens hat im Laufe der Generationen das Standbein zum Fechtbein und das Fechtbein zum Standbein gebogen bzw. zu einem Doppel-Legato verkürzt und gestreckt, eine Haltung, die an die Folies-Bergères gemahnt, aber eher als feudal-antifeudales Relikt anzusprechen ist. Die rückständige Theorie vom gesunkenen Kulturgut verfängt bei ihnen nicht, im Gegenteil, der gelassene Synkretismus, der in der tanzhaften Ausübung ihres Berufszwanges manifest wird, markiert den Schnittpunkt latenter Strömungen vom karpatho-pannonischen zum katalanischen Einflußraum, die beide gewölbt sind, und vice-versa. Erst die Dracula-Version, die sie selber als Mumpitz bezeichnen, verpflanzt ihr Arbeitsgerät in die Salons. Ein objekt-musikalischer Vorgang, der echt ins Herz geht.

If the street sweepers in Reschinar have either two right or two left legs, that means that Reschinar is a long way away from other mountain villages. The swing of their broom over generations has bent their standing leg to their fencing leg or rather shortened and stretched them to a double legato, a pose reminiscent of the Folies Bergères but which should rather be appreciated as a feudal antifeudal relic. The backward theory of sunken culture doesn't work for them, on the contrary, the serene syncretism manifest in the choreographic exercise of their professional compulsion marks the crossroads of latent movements from the Carpatho-Pannonian to the Catalonian sphere of influence, both of which are vaulted, and vice versa. It is the Dracula version, which they themselves refer to as nonsense, which first transplanted their equipment into the salons. A material musical process that really goes to heart.

Von all den Erkenntnisgeschäften, über die ich schlecht Buch führe, sind zwar auch viele abwesend, doch selbst die Vordrucke entbehren fahrlässig der Vollständigkeit.

Of all the epistemological affairs I keep poor records of, many are missing, but even the forms themselves are negligently incomplete.

In der esten zeile stellt sich der dichter ein geschlechts-
organ vor in der zweiten zeile stellt sich der dichter kein
geschlechtsorgan vor in der dritten zeile stellt sich der
dichter vor wie der leser sich ein geschlechtsorgan vorstellt
in der vierten zeile stellt sich der leser vor wie sich ein
geschlechtsorgan den dichter vorstellt in der fünften zeile
stellt sich ein geschlechtsorgan vor wie sich der leser kein
geschlechtsorgan vorstellt in der sechsten zeile stellt sich
der dichter vor wie sich der dichter keinen dichter vorstellt
in der siebenten zeile stellt sich kein leser ein geschlechts-
organ vor in der achten zeile stellt sich kein geschlechtsorgan
vor wie sich kein geschlechtsorgan ein geschlechtsorgan
vorstellt in der neunten zeile stellt sich kein dichter ein
geschlechtsorgan vor in der zehnten zeile stellt ein gesch-
lecht sich ein organ vor das gedicht ist nicht pornografisch
und bezieht seinen reiz aus dem titel NOVEMBER

In the first line the poet imagines a sex organ in the second line the poet imagines the lack of a sex organ in the third line the poet imagines how the reader imagines a sex organ in the fourth line the reader imagines how a sex organ imagines the poet in the fifth line a sex organ imagines how the reader imagines the lack of a sex organ in the sixth line the poet imagines how the poet imagines the lack of a poet in the seventh line the lack of a reader imagines a sex organ in the eighth line the lack of a sex organ imagines how the lack of a sex organ imagines a sex organ in the ninth line the lack of a poet imagines a sex organ in the tenth line a sex imagines an organ this poem is not pornographic and takes its appeal from the title NOVEMBER

Nikolaus Berwanger

(1935–1989)

Berwanger was born on 5 July 1935 in Frreidorf near Timişoara (Temeswar) in Banat. From 1952 to 1969 he worked as an editor for the Bucharest German-language newspaper 'Neuer Weg'. From 1969 to 1984 he was editor-in-chief of the Banat newspaper 'Neuer Banater Zeitung' and became secretary of the Romanian Writers' Union. From 1972 to 1975, a period of political thaw in Romania, he was involved in the literary circle 'Aktionsgruppe Banat' (Banat Action Group). He emigrated to the Federal Republic of Germany in 1984, living in Ludwigsburg near Stuttgart where he died at the beginning of April 1989. He is author of numerous volumes of poetry and prose both in standard German and in Danube Swabian dialect.

in memoriam L.

ein museumsreifes holzkreuz
      ortstafel spurlos verschwunden
      hunde auf wanderschaft
häuser ohne fensterstöcke
      totenköpfe in einem massengrab
kirschen vertrocknen an den ästen
      unten in der heide gabs heuer kaum obst
petroleumlampen ersetzen glühbirnen
      fortschritt wir loben dich
ein familienfoto auf dem dachboden
      fotografisches atelier c. richter aus linz
      wo sind das kernige weib und der
                              erschrockene mann
girlandenfetzen im kulturheim
      die mäuse tanzen eine polka
dorfbibliothek wie eine zelle verriegelt
      nicht nur wegen inventur
ich zieh mit wucht am glockenstrang
      mein appell bleibt unbeantwortet
auf dem friedhof wuchert das gras
      ruhet sanft exbürger von L.
im wohnzimmer starren schafe auf ein
                              christusbild
      geduldige tiere was versteht ihr schon
ein globus und ein geographiebuch im schulhof
      wer zeigt mir morgen wo L. war

In memoriam L.

A wooden cross ready for a museum
    Village sign gone without a trace
    Dogs off a-roaming
Houses bereft of window-sills
    Skulls in a mass grave
Cherries wither on the branches
    Hardly any fruit this year down on the heath
Petroleum lamps instead of lightbulbs
    Progress we praise thee
A family photo in the attic
    Photostudio C. Richter of Linz
    Where are the robust wife and frightened-looking
                                 husband
Remnants of wreaths at the cultural centre
    The mice dancing a polka
Village library locked up like a cell
    Not just for stock-taking
I give a hefty tug at the bell-cord
    My call remains unanswered
Grass covers the cemetery
    Rest in peace, inhabitants of L.
Sheep stare at a picture of Christ in the living-room
    Patient animals what could you possibly understand
A globe and a geography book in the school courtyard
    Who tomorrow will show me where L. was.

Werbetext

die nackte
wahrheit
ist mir
lieber
tausendmal
als die
wintermode 78
im
quellekatalog

Advertisement

I prefer
The naked
Truth
A thousand times over
To the
Winter fashions 1978
In the
Quelle catalogue[1]

---

[1]Quelle: West German mail-order catalogue which circulates at
exorbitant prices in Eastern Europe (transl. note)

Trockene Augen

ehrlich wein ich
nur noch
wenn ich feststelle
daß ein mensch
zum überlaufen
voll ist
mit illusionen
nimmt mir der tod
den besten freund
so heb ich
voller achtung
den hut
meine augen aber
die bleiben trocken

Dry eyes

These days
I cry honestly only
When I see
That someone
Is bursting
With illusions.
When death
Robs me
Of my best friend
I take off
My hat
In respect
But my eyes
Remain dry

Schneewittchen öffne
deine Augen

wir leben
im zeitalter der zwerge
schneewittchen
liegt in einer
intensivstation
die erste geige
weint nur mehr elektronisch
wir leben
im zeitalter der zwerge
schneewittchen
liegt in einer
intensivstation
in unseren seelen
lieben sich
freche krebszellen
wir leben
im zeitalter der zwerge
schneewittchen
liegt in einer
intensivstation
das gewissen zu vieler
ist rein
weil sie es nie benutzen
wir leben
im zeitalter der zwerge
schneewittchen
liegt in einer
intensivstation
die heuchelei
ist unser morgengebet
wir leben
im zeitalter der zwerge
schneewittchen
liegt in einer
intensivstation
wir dürfen zu jeder stunde

einer meinung sein
wir leben
im zeitalter der zwerge
schneewittchen
liegt in einer
intensivstation
riesen zerquetschen uns
wie ameisen
wir leben
im zeitalter der zwerge
schneewittchen
wann öffnest du endlich
deine augen

Snow White
open your eyes

We are living
In an age of dwarfs
Snow White
Is in an
Intensive Care Unit
The first violin
Only weeps electronically now
We are living
In an age of dwarfs
Snow White
Is in an
Intensive Care Unit
Impudent cancer cells
Are making love
In our souls
We are living
In an age of dwarfs
Snow White
Is in an
Intensive Care Unit
The conscience of too many
Is clean
Because they never use it
We are living
In an age of dwarfs
Snow White
Is in an
Intensive Care Unit
Hypocrisy
Is our morning prayer
We are living
In an age of dwarfs
Snow White
Is in an
Intensive Care Unit
We are authorized at any given time

To hold the same opinion
We are living
In an age of dwarfs
Snow White
Is in an
Intensive Care Unit
Giants squash us
Like ants
We are living
In an age of dwarfs
Snow White
When are you finally going
To open your eyes

Absurde Junibilder

die sonne treibt uns tagsüber
den letzten schweißtropfen aus den poren
verschwindet abends ohne reisepaß
in der zollfreien nachtbar einer westmetropole
mit politkabarett aber ohne terroristenschreck
und lacht uns morgens in das verschlafene gesicht

der mond verkündet mit finsterer miene
daß er uns in kürze aus protest
gegen die neokolonialistischen absichten einiger
für lange zeit den rücken kehren wird
was bei der heutigen energieknappheit
sicher zu einer unkontrollierten
bevölkerungsexplosion führen könnte

das große heer der kleinen himmelskörper
probt kurz vor mitternacht
unter der weisen führung des abendsterns
solidarisch den aufstand der glanzproletarier
schon auf der milchstraße geht jeglicher elan verloren
und so bespuckt man aus wut und verzweiflung
kapitalistische und sozialististche flugkörper

die rumänische presseagentur agerpres
ist ermächtigt zu erklären
daß jedes land
unabhängig von seiner größe oder stärke
das heilige recht hat
seine inneren angelegenheiten
ohne eine intervention von außen zu lösen

ferner wird verlautet
daß das großkombinat morgenröte
zuständig für die industrialisierte herstellung
von scheuklappen aller farbtönungen
bei totalem verzicht auf importe
sein gegenüber dem vergangenen planjahrfünft
verdreifachtes soll
vcorfristig erfüllt ja sogar überboten hat

Images of an absurd June

During the day the sun squeezes
The last drops of sweat out of our pores
And slips out in the evening without a passport
To the duty-free nightclub of a Western metropolis,
With political cabaret but no terrorist threat
And laughs in our drowsy faces the next morning.

The moon announces with a sombre countenance
That it intends to turn its back on us
For quite a while soon in protest against
The neo-colonialist intentions of some,
Which, given the scarcity of energy nowadays,
Could no doubt lead to an
Uncontrollable population explosion.

Just before midnight the great army
Of tiny celestial bodies rehearses an uprising,
Its solidarity with the glorious proletariat,
Under the sage leadership of the evening star.
On the Milky Way all the drive peters out
And in anger and desperation they spit at
Capitalist and socialist space ships.

The Romanian News Agency Agerpres
Is authorized to announce
That every country
Independent of its size and strength
Has the sacred right
To solve its internal affairs
Without intervention from abroad.

It goes on to state
That Sunrise Industries,
Responsible for the manufacture
Of blinkers in all hues and colours,
Has fulfilled production limits
Ahead of schedule by three times over
Those of the last five-year plan,
Without relying on imports at all.

Ehrlich

es ist kein lippenbekenntnis auf bestellung
ich liebe dieses land ehrlich

mit seiner kindischen unreife
mit seiner neigung zur selbstverherrlichung
mit seiner ungezähmtheit
und ich verzeih alles
weil man hier noch verzeihen kann

Späte Freude

deine umarmung
hat ein seltenes
bukett
erinnerungen
an trauben
geerntet
nach dem ersten reif
werden in mir wach

Honestly

It is no made-to-order lip service
I honestly love this country

With its childish immaturity
With its inclination to self-glorification
With its untamedness
And I pardon it all
Because you can still pardon here

Late joy

Your embrace
Has a rare
Bouquet
Memories
Are aroused within me
Of grapes
Harvested
After the first frost

Claus Stephani

(1938–)

Writer and poet from Brașov (Kronstadt) in Transylvania. He was born on 25 July 1938 and studied German language and literature in Bucharest (1960–1965) and thereafter journalism. He was deputy editor in chief of the Bucharest German-language literary magazine 'Neue Literatur'. Stephani is also a well-known ethnographer and has published a number of volumes of German-Romanian folk tales.

Marmatien (I)

Tritt achtsam ein
in dies Land
wo Regengewölk
und Wind
unterm
rauchigen Dach
der Berge
hausen
wo Hunde
tags
auf der Schwelle
im leichten Schlaf
knurren
und Wölfe
im letzten Herbstlicht
schon
den Winter melden
wo Mädchen
kommend
aus den weiten Häusern
der Wälder
ihre Knie
waschen
abends
am dunklen Fluß
Wischau
Tritt achtsam ein
in dies stille Land
das Echo
deiner Worte
folgt dir
springt dich
schweigst du
an

Marmatia[1] (excerpt)

Enter this land
Cautiously
Where rainclouds
And wind
Under the
Smoky roof
Of mountains
Make their home
Where dogs
By day
Growl
In their slumber
In doorways
And wolves
In the last light of autumn
Report
The arrival of winter
Where girls
Coming
From distant forest
Homes
Wash
Their knees
In the evening
At the dark river
Wischau
Enter this silent land
Cautiously
The echo
Of your words
Is following you
Will pounce
Be you silent
Upon you

---

[1] Marmatia: Latin name for the Maramureş district of northern
Romania (Transl. note).

Biographie

Wenn du vernünftig bist
sagte Vater
kaufe ich dir
einen neuen Himmel

Wenn du vernünftig bist
sagte Marie
darfst du
meine Blumen hüten

Wenn du vernünftig bist
sagte der Genosse
lege ich dir
einen Selbstlaut ins Ohr

Wenn Sie ein bißschen vernünftiger
leben
sagte der Arzt
(er sagte es kühl und
im fortgeschrittenen Alter)
leben Sie
noch lang

Seither
lebe ich lang

Biography

If you are sensible
Said father
I'll buy you
A new heaven

If you are sensible
Said Mary
You may
Look after my flowers

If you are sensible
Said the comrade
I'll place
A vowel in your ear

If you live a bit more
Sensibly
Said the doctor
(saying it calmly and
At an advanced age)
You will live
For a long time

Since then
I've been living for a long time

Pompei, via Stabiana

Täglich
warten die Steine
auf vorgebuchte Touristen

Die kommen pünktlich
um zehn
mit schönen Hunden
und teuren Frauen
die einen pissen
die Säulen an
die andern lächeln
Kameras klicken

Um elf fährt ab der Bus
zurück bleibt die Antike
still und standhaft

Pompeii, via Stabiana

Day after day
The stones await
Pre-booked tourists

Who arrive at ten
On the dot
With beautiful dogs
And expensive wives
Some piss
On the columns
Others smile
Cameras click

At eleven the bus departs
Antiquity is left behind
Silent and steadfast.

Poesie Club

Sag mir wer
dein Kritiker ist
und ich sag dir wer
du bist
oder:
Sag mir mit wem
du umgehst
und ich sag dir
woran es liegt

Poetry Club

Tell me who
Your critic is
And I'll tell you who
You are
Or:
Tell me who
You keep company with
And I'll tell you
The reason why

Siebenbürgische Kirchenburg

Logis
für Fledermäuse die
ohne Genehmigung
in den Achselhöhlen der Mauern
wie offne Regenschirme
hängen
Kommen Touristen
häkeln sie
leise lachend
aus Taubenmist
ihre Legenden

Fortified church in Transylvania

Lodgings
For bats
Hanging
Unauthorized
Like open umbrellas
In the armpits of walls.
When tourists come by
They crochet
Their legends,
Laughing softly,
With pigeon manure.

Albrecht Janesch '90

Anemone Latzina

(1942–)

Latzina was born in Braşov (Kronstadt) in Transylvania on 17 February 1942 and studied German language and literature in Bucharest from 1962 to 1967. Since 1969, she has been working for the German-language literary magazine 'Neue Literatur' in Bucharest where she presently resides. She is the author of much verse and translations from Romanian, Hungarian, English, French and Bulgarian.

Am Morgen

Am Morgen dusche ich mir
die Nacht vom Körper.
Ich will es mir unbequem machen.
Ich höre Radio.
Ich höre Radio.
Ich höre Radio.

Am Morgen schminke ich mir
das Dunkel aus dem Gesicht.
Ich will es mir unbequem machen.
Ich lese die Zeitung.
Ich lese die Zeitung.
Ich lese die Zeitung.

Am Morgen kämme ich mir
die Träume aus dem Haar.
Ich will es mir unbequem machen.
Ich seh mir die Leute an.
Ich seh mir die Leute an.
Ich seh mir die Leute an.

In the morning

In the morning I shower
The night from my body.
I want to make it difficult for myself.
I listen to the radio.
I listen to the radio.
I listen to the radio.

In the morning I paint
The darkness out of my face.
I want to make it difficult for myself.
I read the newspaper.
I read the newspaper.
I read the newspaper.

In the morning I comb
The dreams out of my hair.
I want to make it difficult for myself.
I take a look at the people.
I take a look at the people.
I take a look at the people.

13. Juli 1974

mädchen hab ich heute morgen (Frieder nennt
mich so) zu mir gesagt unter der dusche bei
m zähneputzen mädchen jetzt hast du schon d
eine vierten zähne (milchzähne wasserzähne bi
erzähne schnapszähne) und außerdem war d
er blonde Peter gestern bei dir und hat ge
sagt er will eine anthologie machen und du
sollst ihm gedichte schicken die ER AUCH V
eröffentlichen KANN die mußt du aber erst
machen also schreib dem blonden Peter ein g
edicht übers ALTWERDEN das ist doch ein the
ma wenn man über dreißig ist (man muß jung
genug sein damit man übers altwerden was sa
gen kann) also mädchen du wirst langsam alt
sag ich und denk das könnte ein gedicht wer
den oder besser noch ein SCHLAGER oder sons
twas aber da sitz ich schon in der straßenb
ahn und da kommt eine Frau so an stupst mic
h und sagt mach platz (ich dachte mit dem k
urzen haar hält dich doch keiner fürn junge
n) bürschchen damit ich meine tasche hinste
ll und UNTERBRICHT mich in meinen schöns
ten gedanken übers altwerden jetzt sind sie for
t jetzt kann ich nichts mehr übers altwerde
n sagen diese frau hat mir ALLES VERMASS
ELT und überhaupt wie soll man noch irgend
was über irgendwas sagen wenn immerzu einer
daherkommt und einem DIE SCHÖNSTEN G
EDANKEN VERMASSELT . . .

13 July 1974

Gal (as Frieder calls me) I said to my
self this morning in the shower brushi
ng my teeth gal you're now on to your
fourth set of teeth (milk-teeth water-
teeth beer-teeth schnaps-teeth) and an
yway Peter that blond guy was here yes
terday and said he wanted to do an ant
hology and you should send him some po
ems he can PUBLISH but you've gotta wr
ite them first OK write a poem for Pet
er that blond guy on GROWING OLD that'
s a good subject when you're over thir
ty (you've got to be young enough to h
ave something to say about growing old
) OK gal I say you're not getting any
younger and think this could be a poem
or better still a HIT or something but
I'm already sitting in the streetcar a
nd this woman comes along and nudges m
e and says move over (I didn't think w
ith my short hair that anyone would ta
ke me for a) young man so I can put my
bag down and INTERRUPTS me in my best
ideas about growing old now they're go
ne now I can't say anything about grow
ing old this woman has BOTCHED UP EVER
YTHING and how are you supposed to say
anything about anything anyway when so
omeone always comes along and BOTCHES U
P THE BEST IDEAS . . .

Klagefragen nach allem was ich an diese weite Welt verloren

Wo sind meine Fingernägel,
abgeschnitten im Hotel „Royal", Budapest?
Hat die Donau sie weggeschwemmt?
Oh und meine vielen Kippen,
geraucht Schillerstraße 16,
in Freiburg im Breisgau?
Was ist aus den Flaschen „Perrier" geworden,
getrunken in der ersten Etage „Residence Lyon",
nicht weit von der Place de la Bastille?
Am Strand von Yalta,
die Schuppen meiner verbrannten Haut,
liegt noch eine Spur zwischen den Steinen?
Die Zwiebelschalen
auf den Kanälen von Amsterdam, von Venedig,
ob meine noch mitschwimmen?
In Tallinn hab ich einen Bleistift verloren,
schreibt wohl jemand damit?
Wer weiß von den faulen Bananen,
die ich in Rom, Campo di fiori,
zu den Marktresten geworfen?
Meine Fahrkarten der Wiener Straßenbahn
wurden, wo wohl, zu Asche?
Und meine Hühneraugen in der Badewanne in Brüssel?
Und meine Spuren im Hamburger Schnee?
Werden die Rechnungen des Café Odéon, Zürich,
                                      aufbewahrt?
Was wurde aus meiner Zahnplombe im Weißbrot von
                                         Nizza?
Was wird aus meinem Haar,
im Müllschlucker von „The May Flower", Iowa City,
                                    USA, versenkt?
Und meine zarten Knochen, meine zerrauchten Lungen,
meine durchtrunkene Leber –
wo werden die verwesen?

Lament for all I've lost
to this wide world

Where are the fingernails
I cut at the Hotel Royal, Budapest?
Has the Danube carried them away?
Oh, and the butts of the many cigarettes
I smoked at Schillerstrasse 16
In Freiburg im Breisgau?
What happened to the bottles of Perrier
Drunk on the first floor of the Residence Lyon
Not far from Place de la Bastille?
Do traces of my peeling skin
Still linger among the stones
On the beach at Yalta?
The onion skins
In the canals of Amsterdam and Venice,
Are mine still floating there with the rest?
I lost a pencil in Tallinn,
Is someone else using it?
Who knows what happened to the rotten bananas
I threw into the garbage in Rome
At the Campo dei Fiori market.
Have my tickets for the Vienna streetcar
Now turned to ash? I wonder where.
And my corns in a bathtub in Brussels?
And my footprints in the Hamburg snow?
Are my bills from the Café Odeon in Zurich still being
                                                    kept?
What happened to the filling I lost in the French bread in
                                                    Nice?
What has happened to the hair I dumped
Into the garbage shoot at the May Flower in Iowa City,
                                                    USA?

And my tender bones, my charred lungs,
My saturated liver,
Where will they rot?

Im Juli 1977

denn jetzt steht es fest
in dieser großen freiheit
das gedicht ist ein gefängnis
in seinen zellen hocken
verdächtige figuren, stilfiguren,
zwielichtige gedanken
verkommene bilder
unter ihnen auch spitzel,
die satzzeichen,
ein fragezeichen genügt
und eine verschwörung fliegt auf
ja ja das gedicht ist ein gefängnis
und wir sind lebenslänglich
dazu verurteilt
uns bei ihm zu holen
was man so zum leben braucht
wasser und brot

In July 1977

It's an established fact now
A poem is a prison
In this great freedom of ours,
In its cell sit
Suspicious figures, figures of speech,
Shady thoughts,
Seedy images
Among them are informers too,
The punctuation marks,
A question mark is enough
To uncover a plot,
Yes, a poem is a prison
And we are sentenced
For life
To take from it
What we need to survive,
Bread and water.

Frieder Schuller

(1942–)

Born in Caţa (Katzendorf) near Braşov
(Kronstadt) in Transylvania, Schuller
studied theology and German in Sibiu
(Hermannstadt) and Cluj (Klausenburg).
From 1968 to 1972 he was cultural editor
of the German-language weekly
'Karpaten Rundschau' and from 1972 to
1978 worked for the German section of
the Sibiu (Hermannstadt) State Theatre.
He now lives in the Federal Republic of
Germany and is the author of three
volumes of verse.

Altweibersommer im Kaufhaus

Altweibersommer im Kaufhaus
Früchte fallen auf Rolltreppen
das Laub in die Kassen

billig stirbt
was mir teuer ist

wühlen lä'ßt sich auch in Kisten
voller Schiller Heine Mörike Hebbel
Klassikerausgaben funkelnagelneu
in eigenem Stall desinfiziert
und aus der DDR auf die BRD losgelassen

Wertarbeit deutsch und ungeteilt
gottseidank tot
so kamen sie preiswert über die Grenzen.

Indian summer in a department store

Indian summer in a department store
Fruit falling on escalator
Leaves into cash registers

Cheaply dies
What is dear to me.

Rummaging around in boxes
Full of Schiller, Heine, Mörike, Hebbel
Editions of classics, brand new
Disinfected in their own stall
And released by the East upon the West

Quality work, German and undivided
And dead thank God
That's how they got across the border cheaply.

Vielleicht meine Kaffeeschale

Vielleicht meine kaffeeschale
wenn es hieße
es ist soweit
würde ich mitnehmen
denn für alles andere
nimmt sich die Erinnerung grausam Zeit.
Dies wäre mein Gedicht
hingeschrieben für die bewölkte Stunde
ich bekäme plötzlich den Paß
nach Westdeutschland oder überhaupt.

Perhaps I'd take my coffee mug

Perhaps I'd take my coffee mug
If suddenly
The time came
To go
Because memory takes
Its gruesome time for everything else.
This would be my poem,
Jotted down for the cloudy day
When I suddenly got my passport
For West Germany or anywhere.

Franz
Hodjak

(1944–)

Born in Sibiu (Hermannstadt) in Tran-
sylvania on 27 September 1944, Hodjak
studied German language and literature
in Cluj-Napoca (Klausenburg) where he
presently works for Dacia publishing
company. He is a prolific writer of verse
and is also author of prose, children's
literature and translations from Hun-
garian and Romanian.

Spielräume

die freiheit
die täglich
uns spielraum
gewährt
ist immer so groß wie
der spielraum
den täglich
wir der freiheit
gewähren

Scope

The freedom
Which gives us
Scope
Day by day
Is always as great
As the scope
We give
To freedom
Day by day

Reiner Kunze

er ist nicht kranführer
versteht nichts von schweißverfahren
auch hält er in der hand
keine kelle

und doch

die baustellen sind ihm
nicht fremd

und doch

was er baut baut er nur langsam
er baut auf vertrauen

er hilft mit
von der gegenseite des lichts:

wo im schatten der
gerüste
zuweilen noch hochschießt
zählebiges unkraut
mit viel geschrei

dort
geht er umher

geht zu jäten
mit zweischneidigem wort

Reiner Kunze[1]

He is not a crane operator,
He knows nothing of welding methods
Nor does he hold a trowel
In his hand

And yet

Construction sites
Are not foreign to him

And yet

What he builds, he builds slowly,
He builds on trust

He helps
From the other side of the light:

Where in the shadow
Of the scaffolding
Tenacious weeds
Still shoot up
With much ado

There
He putters about

Weeding
With the double-edged word.

[1]Reiner Kunze (1933—); German poet and writer (transl. note).

Im Friedhof

lesend auf den grabsteinen
all die namen all der guten
die von uns geschieden
frage ich

wo nur liegen die bösen
oder leben die ewig unter uns?

At the cemetery

Reading on the tombstones
The names of all the good people
Who have departed this life,
I wonder

Where are the bad ones buried,
Or do they live on eternally among us?

Ratschlag

seid vorsichtig im umgang
mit büchern

geht auf die straße
betretet die werkhallen
fahrt mit der straßenbahn
besucht die versammlungen
besucht die museen
geht auf die ämter
geht in die läden

entziffert die blicke
studiert die gewohnheiten
lest die träume
lernt das schweigen richtig übersetzen
studiert die grüße
lest die kardiogramme
lest in den gesichtern

traut nicht den wahrheiten
aus zweiter hand

Advice

Be careful in dealing
With books

Go out into the street
Enter the factories
Take the streetcar
Attend meetings
Visit museums
Go into offices
Go into shops

Decipher glances
Study habits
Read dreams
Learn to interpret silence properly
Study greetings
Read cardiograms
Read faces

Do not trust
Second-hand truths

Ovid im Exil

vergessen von den sieben hügeln vom hohen himmel
über dem tiber von den schatten der pinien vergessen
von den festlichen gärten aus dem gedächtnis gewischt
des forum romanum aufgegeben von kennern und
                                                                        gönnern
verlassen vom letzten funken glück von ruf und
namen verlassen von jeder hoffnung verlassen
selbst vom allerletzten vom humor

treu blieben allein die feinde

Ovid in exile[1]

Forgotten by the seven hills by the lofty skies
Over the Tiber by the shadows of the pinetrees forgotten
By the festive gardens erased from the memory
Of the Roman forum forsaken by connoisseurs and
                                              patrons
Abandoned by the last spark of joy by name and
Reputation abandoned by all hope abandoned even
By the ultimate, by humour

Only enemies remain faithful

---

[1]The Roman poet Ovid (43BC–17AD) was sent into exile in 9AD to Tomis
(Constanza) on the Black Sea where he died (transl. note).

Nach der Lektüre von Gedichten Weinhebers im Rückblick auf seinen Erfolg in den Dreissigerjahren

seine gedichte sagen viel
seine gedichte verschweigen viel

wofür wurden seine gedichte honoriert?

Über alle Grenzen hinweg

Wulf Kirsten und ich trinken ein bier,
er in Weimar, ich hier.

Upon reading poems by Weinheber in view of his success in the Thirties[1]

His poems say a lot
His poems leave a lot unsaid

Why were his poems honoured?

Transcending borders

Wulf Kirsten and I are drinking beer,
He's in Weimar and I am here.

[1] Josef Weinheber (1892–1945); Austrian lyric poet (transl. note).

Villons Ankunft im Himmel

geehrte kommission
ich fühle mich wie neugeboren

während der reise wurde ich von engelsflügeln geschüttelt
bis zum totalen verlust des bewußtseins

vorschriftsmäßig habe ich fünf volle wochen gewartet
in zugigen treppenhäusern ungeheizten hallen und korridoren

schließlich wurde ich eingelassen über die hintertreppe
durch die türe des dienstpersonals

ein heiliger wahrscheinlich achten ranges brachte mich
in eine zweistöckige wolke neubarocken stils

ich wurde nach unerwünschten erdendingen abgesucht
bis auf den grund meiner umgestülpten seele

wie aus einem lautsprecher drangen aus einer kapuze
in sphärischer tonlage die neuen zehn gebote

mit zehn mal zehn langstieligen gladiolen
habe ich gewissenhaft alle fragebogen ausgefüllt

beim verlassen des bades tauschte ich den geruchssinn
gegen einen breitkrempigen glorienschein

an allen betten erschienen auf großen regenschirmen
szenen aus dem neunten kreis der hölle

fünf kronleuchter durchschauten gleich meinen ersten traum
in dem ich versehentlich mit der dicken Margot gesprochen

der eintritt in den berühmten säulengang im myrtenhain
blieb mir versagt wegen der allzu kurzen flügel

im amt der wetterprognosen ging es ganz lustig zu
wir drehten tüten aus unseren trommelfellen

mein rechtes auge ließ ich einmontieren als linse
in das allgegenwärtige gottesteleskop

das andere schließlich habe ich freiwillig gespendet
für die vollkommenheit meines eignen glücks

meine herren ich bewundre ehrlich ihre himmlische ordnung
deshalb glaube ich meine anwesenheit hier ist ein irrtum

ich bitte zu bedenken ich hartgesottener lump
könnte eines tags unter der last dieser güte zerbrechen

Villon's arrival in heaven[1]

Esteemed Commission
I feel reborn.

During the trip I was so shaken by angel wings
That I completely lost conscience.

I waited the prescribed five full weeks
In draughty stairwells, unheated hallways and corridors.

I was finally let in up the back stairs
Through the staff entrance.

A saint, probably of the eighth degree, took me
Into a two-storey Neo-Baroque cloud.

I was searched for unwelcome earthly goods,
Turned inside out to the very bottom of my soul.

Out of a cowl, as if from a loudspeaker,
Issued the new ten commandments in a celestial pitch.

With ten times ten long-stemmed gladioli
I filled out all the forms to the best of my ability.

On leaving the bath I exchanged my sense of smell
For a broad-brimmed halo.

Scenes from the ninth circle of hell
Appeared at all the beds on large umbrellas.

Five candelabra immediately saw through my first dream
In which I accidently spoke to fat Margot.

I was refused entry into the famous colonnade
In the myrtle grove because of my short wings.

At the meteorological office we had great fun
Making bags out of our eardrums.

I had my right eye installed as a lens
For God's omnipresent telescope.

The other I donated voluntarily
For the perfection of my own bliss.

Gentlemen, I am honestly amazed at your heavenly order,
I therefore regard my presence here as an error.

I would ask you to consider that I might one day, scoundrel
That I am, collapse under the weight of your kindness.

[1] François Villon (1431–1463); French poet (Transl. note).

Autobiographie

genosse, was habe ich
anzuführen?

geboren wurde ich
bei verdunklung und ausgangsverbot

kurz darauf wurde das haus enteignet

daß ich die Expressionisten mag oder pralle brüste
ist sicher wesentlicher
als die vergangenheit
der verwandten

die schulen hab ich alle
nach vierundvierzig besucht

aufschlußreicher als alle mitgliedschaften
sind, glaube ich
meine Bücher

engere kontakte unterhalte ich
zur aufklärung, zu meerlandschaften, zu den verlorenen
illusionen

abends höre ich nachrichten
die politische lage interessiert mich tatsächlich

einen festen wohnsitz hab ich bloß
als empfänger von stromrechnungen, zeitungen
honoraren
vorladungen

woran ich glaube? an keine seligkeit
weder der aufrüstung noch der auferstehung

sehen Sie, der horizont ist diesig
wie Ihre vorstellung
von mir

Autobiography

Comrade,
What can I say?

I was born
At curfew time during the blackout

Shortly afterwards the house was expropriated

That I like the Expressionists and firm breasts
Is doubtless more important
Than the past
Of my relatives

All the schools I attended
Were after nineteen forty-four

More revealing than all my memberships,
I believe, are
My books

I maintain close contacts
With the enlightenment, seascapes and lost illusions

In the evening I listen to the news,
I really am interested in politics

I maintain a fixed address
Simply to get electricity bills, newspapers,
Royalties,
Summonses

What I believe in? Not in salvation
Either by the arms build-up or by resurrection

You see, the horizon is hazy
Just like your ideas
About me.

Savonarola

wie lautlos fallen die entscheidungen!
während du ahnungslos die zeitung liest,
schließen sich vielleicht schon
um deine knöchel unsichtbare ringe.

sprich aus die richtung deiner gedanken!
du weißt, du bist stark bloß als gegner.
die stille, sie zimmert kreuze,
und langsam wächst dir das gras in den mund.

Savonarola[1]

How silently decisions are made!
As you obliviously read your newspaper
Invisible rings are perhaps already
Closing around your ankles.

Speak the direction of your thoughts!
You know that you are only strong as an adversary.
Silence is a carpenter of crosses,
And the grass is gradually growing in your mouth.

[1]Girolamo Savonarola (1452–1498); Dominican monk and political
leader in Renaissance Florence (transl. note).

Alltag

jeder tag ist ein
buch

darin blättern wir nach
bildern

abends legen wirs beiseite
ungelesen

Daily routine

Each day is a
Book

We flip through it
Looking for pictures

In the evening we put it away
Unread

Rolf Frieder Marmont

(1944–)

Marmont was born in Braşov (Kron-
stadt) in Transylvania on 4 December
1944. He studied German and English
in Bucharest from 1963 to 1968 and has
worked there as a speaker for Radio
Bucharest and as reader for Kriterion
publishing company. On 11th April
1988, he emigrated to the Federal Re-
public of Germany and now works for a
publishing company in Hanover.

Geräumige Sekunden

Sekunden
sind groß
wie Scheunen,
in denen viele Wagenladungen Leben
Platz finden:

Im hohen Norden irgendwo
füttert ein alter Eskimo seine hungrigen Hunde.
In einer Mansarde
kämmt singend eine Frau ihr Haar.
Ein Fischer sieht verträumt
in seine wieder leeren Netze.
Ein Knabe schreibt seiner Geliebten.
Ein Kind weint.
Ein Baum stirbt ab.
Ein anderer treibt Knospen.
Der Dichter
vergißt seine Gedichte.
Andere streiken.
Die Waagschale der Nacht
steigt langsam höher.
Am Fischmarkt zanken ältliche Schlampen.

Sekunden sind groß
wie Scheunen.

Spacious seconds

Seconds
Are as big
As barns
With room for truckloads
Of life:

Somewhere up in the far north
An old Eskimo is feeding his hungry dogs.
In a mansard
A woman is combing her hair and singing.
A fisherman is staring dreamily
Into his empty nets again.
A boy is writing to his girlfriend.
A child is crying.
A tree is dying.
Another is blossoming.
The poet
Is forgetting his poems.
Others are on strike.
The scales of night
Are slowly rising.
Slovenly old hags are bickering at the fish market.

Seconds are as big
As barns.

Schattenreich Dobrudscha

Müder Landstrich,
entblößt von Historie.
Im Fadenkreuz nicht viel mehr als
gläserne Disteln
zwischen Dünenbuckeln
und Stille,
sonnendurchglüht.

Hinter den Horizont
kippt ein Knäuel Möwen,
mit ihnen deutsche Laute,
Mutter und *Vater*.
Was bleibt, ist die
unerschütterliche Dialektik
pontischer Brandung,
allmächtiger einschläfernder Singsang.

Spürst auch du, Bruder,
den Zungenknebel im Mund,
das Sandkorn unterm Lid,
den feinen Stich in der Brust?

Dobruja[1] realm of shade

Weary land,
Divested of history.
In the web of things not much more than
Thistles of glass
Between the dunes
And silence,
Sun-drenched.

A bevy of gulls
Plunges behind the horizon,
Accompanied by German sounds,
'Mutter' and 'Vater'.
What remains
Are the unshakeable dialectics
Of Pontian surf,
An omnipotent and soporific singsong.

Can you too, brother,
Feel the gag in your mouth,
The grain of sand under your eyelid,
The subtle pang in your chest?

[1]Dobruja: area of Romania between the lower Danube and the
Black Sea (transl. note).

Kinder

Sie kamen am Morgen,
Mit kleinen Händen
Den Weinberg
Nach Schnecken zu durchstöbern.

Trafen aber nur
Auf etliche Silbermünzen,
Römische.

Hängenden Hauptes
Kehrten sie abends heim.

Children

They came in the morning
With little hands
To comb the vineyards
For snails

But found only
A few silver coins,
Roman ones.

Hanging their heads
They returned home in the evening.

Johann Lippet

(1951–)

Lippett was born in Wels, Austria on 12 January 1951. In 1956, his family returned to Romania. From 1970 to 1974 he studied German language and literature in Timişoara (Temeswar) where he was a member of the literary circle 'Aktionsgruppe Banat' (Banat Action Group). He also taught German for several years and was active at the German State Theatre in Timişoara. In 1987 he emigrated to the Federal Republic of Germany and lives presently in Heidelberg.

Gewesener Selbstmordgang der Familie
(frei nach meiner Urgroßmutter und meiner Großmutter)

und ich glaube
daß ihr bewußtsein
sich gewandelt hat
da sie an feiertagen
die bäume weißen
und fahnen heraushängen
lange zeit hatten sie keine fahnen
als die todesfahne
die an der kirche hing
wenn jemand gestorben war
und sie war schwarz die fahne
man sagte
der selbstmord sei in der familie
weil viele selbstmord begangen haben
die tochter des bruders
meiner urgroßmutter
erhängte sich aus liebe für einen mann
alle die selbstmord begangen haben
in unserer familie
erhängten sich
es erhängte sich
mein urgroßvater
er war husar gewesen
erzählte mir meine urgroßmutter
er erhängte sich
als einer ihm ins gesicht schlug
als man ihm seine eggen pflüge und seine sämaschine
wegnahm
die er sich aus der schweiz hat schicken lassen
sagte meine urgroßmutter
er nahm den strick
hielt seine zeit damit fest
und sie beerdigten ihn
weil sie dem arzt zwei zentner weizen geschenkt hatten
und er ein christliches todeszeugnis ausstellte
erzählte meine urgroßmutter
es erhängte sich

ein anderes mädchen der familie
auch aus liebe
und sie beerdigten sie
als jungfrau
sie war auf den strümpfen
vom ball nach hause gelaufen
weil die eltern den jungen nicht wollten
mit dem sie getanzt hatte
sie nahm den strick
und hielt ihre liebe damit fest
es erhängte sich
ein anderer aus der familie
wie mir großmutter erzählte
weil er müde war
er durchschnitt sich mit dem großen messer die venen
er erhängte sich mit durchgeschnittenen venen
er nahm das große messer und den strick
und hielt seine müdigkeit damit fest
es erhängten sich
noch drei aus der familie
sie waren schon alt
sie nahmen den strick
und hielten ihr alter damit fest
ich glaube daß sich jetzt
ihr bewußtsein gewandelt hat
seit jahrzehnten
hat sich keiner mehr erhängt
für eggen pflüge sämaschinen
aus liebe
aus müdigkeit
aus alter
sie weißen ihre bäume an feiertagen
und hängen fahnen heraus

Onetime spate of suicides in the family
(according to my great-grandmother and my grandmother)

And I believe
There's been
A change of thinking among them
Because they whitewash the trees
On holidays
And hang out flags,
For a long time
They had no other flag
But the flag of death
Hanging from the church when someone had died,
And the flag was black.
They said
Suicide ran in the family
Because many of them had committed suicide,
The daughter of the brother
Of my great-grandmother
Hanged herself out of love for a man,
All those who've committed suicide
In our family
Have hanged themselves,
My great-grandfather
Hanged himself,
He was a hussar
So my great-grandmother told me,
He hanged himself
When someone punched him the face
And they took away the ploughs, harrows and the seeder
He had ordered from Switzerland,
So my great-grandmother told me,
He took a rope
And held his time fast with it
And they buried him
Because they'd given the doctor two hundredweight of
$\qquad$ wheat
And he signed a Christian death certificate,
So my great-grandmother said,
Another girl in the family

Hanged herself
Out of love
And they buried her
A virgin,
She had run home from the dance
In her stockings
Because her parents didn't like the boy
She'd been dancing with,
She took a rope
And held her love fast with it,
Someone else in the family
Hanged himself,
So grandmother told me,
Because he was tired,
He severed his veins with a big knife
And hanged himself with severed veins,
He took a big knife and rope
And held his weariness fast with it,
Three other people in the family
Hanged themselves,
They were already old,
They took a rope
And held their old age fast with it,
I believe there's now been
A change of thinking among them,
No one's hanged himself
For decades
Because of ploughs, harrows, seeders
Out of love
Out of weariness
Out of old age,
They whitewash their trees on holidays
And hang out flags.

Mein Nachbar macht mir ein Gedicht

„dir gehts gut",
sagt mein nachbar,
„du hast zeit, nachzudenken über das leben,
über deine sorgen und hoffnungen führst du buch,
du kannst dir ein gedicht machen für deine freuden
und traurige worte schreiben über deine enttäuschungen,
herauswinden kannst du dich durch eine wendung,
wenn man dir zu viele fragen stellt."

ja, ich gebe zu:
das leben wird schwerer,
leichter der tod.

My neighbour makes a poem for me

'You're lucky,'
Says my neigbour,
'You've got time on your hands to think about life,
You can keep accounts of your worries and expectations.
You can write a poem for your own pleasure
Or words of sorrow on your disappointments.
You can extricate yourself with the turn of a phrase
If they ask too many questions.'

Yes, I admit
Life is getting more difficult,
Death is getting easier.

Wochenende Der Kopf

an diesem wochenendnachmittag
steigt mein nachbar die treppen des stiegenhauses hoch,
im einkaufsnetz einen schweinskopf.
der rüssel durchwühlt das land.

Weekend. The head

On this weekend afternoon
My neighbour trudges up the steps of the stairwell
With a pig's head in his shopping net.
The snout rummages through the land.

Auch. Eine ars poetica

immer wieder genötigt, geständnisse abzulegen
– schmerzhafter ist es, den nagel aus dem fleisch zu ziehen,
als ihn sich ins fleisch jagen zu lassen –,
immer wieder genötigt, sich selbst aufzugeben
– fröstelnder erwartet man den abend
als das krähen des hahns im morgengrauen –,
immer wieder genötigt, neu zu beginnen
– beängstigender sind meine täglichen gedanken
als die ausgesprochenen sätze

beim ablegen der geständnisse,
beim sich-selbst-aufgeben,
beim neuen beginnen –,

immer wieder genötigt, sich zu rechtfertigen,
tödlicher.

Also. An Ars Poetica

Always being forced to make confessions
(it is more painful to extract the nail from your flesh
Than to have it hammered in),
Always being forced to relinquish oneself
(more chilling awaiting evening
Than the cock's crowing at dawn),
Always being forced to begin again
(more frightening are my daily thoughts
Than that which is said

In making confessions,
In relinquishing one's self,
In beginning again),

Always being forced to justify oneself.
More lethal.

Jeden Abend
sammeln sich meine Gedanken
vor der Tür.
Dann ziehen sie die Schuhe aus,
damit sie geräuschlos
und ohne Schmutz zu machen
bis zu mir kommen können.
Ich betrachte sie:
ihre Schönheit,
die Eleganz ihrer idealen Körper,
und öffne dann rasch das Fenster.
Während ich vor der Tür
die vom Schmutz beladenen Schuhe einsammle,
weichen die Idealbilder durchs Fenster.

Every evening
My thoughts collect
At the door.
Then they take their shoes off
So that they can come to me
Silently
Without making any dirt.
I watch them,
Their beauty,
The elegance of their ideal bodies,
And then quickly open the window.
Through the window escape the ideal visions
While I pick up the dirty shoes
At the door.

Werner Söllner

(1951–)

Söllner was born in Horia (Neupanat) near Arad and studied physics, German and English in Cluj-Napoca (Klausenburg). He worked for a publishing company in Bucharest until 1982 when he emigrated to the Federal Republic of Germany. He presently lives in Frankfurt. Söllner is the author of seven volumes of verse published in Romania and Germany.

Leben. Ein Beispiel

Da fällt mir ein Buch in die Hände
mit Bildern und Fotografien Nâzim Hikmets:

Nâzim der Revolutionär, unrasiert, einen groben
Wollschal um den Hals geschlungen; Nâzim mit
                              russischen
Ballettmeistern (lernt er wohl den Wechselschritt
durch die Geschichte?); Nâzim als Kind; Nâzim als junger
Seekadett auf den Prinzeninseln; Nâzim in kriegerischer
Stimmung in Anatolien; Nâzim
bei seinen Freunden im Ausland, friedlich
auf Reisen, auf der Flucht vor Kemal; Nâzim
als Sonnentrinker im Gefängnis von Hopa
von Bursa, von Istanbul, Çankiri, wieder
von Bursa; Nâzim im Hungerstreik, Nâzim
bricht das Brot seiner Freiheit
mit Paul Robeson, Julius Fučik und Pablo Neruda
(sie alle sind schon lange tot); Nâzim
auf des Flucht über das Schwarze
Meer, in Moskau, Berlin, in
Sofia und Peking, in Polen
wenig ahnend, in der Tschechoslowakei und in Ungarn,
                              in Frankreich;
Nâzim mit zerrissenem Herzen in Erwartung des Todes
schreibt in Prag das Stundenbuch neu, erlebt seinen
ersten Abend in Rom, fragt rätselhaft nach
Paris, berichtet aus Havanna, genießt die Nachteile
des Exils, beschreibt die Revolutionäre
als Romantiker (was hätte Nâzim wohl in einer wirklichen
Revolution getan?); Nâzim rasiert sich
vor dem Spiegel, Nâzim freut sich an der Natur, verliebt sich
mit sechzig, Nâzim kocht, ist ernst
liest Zeitung, Nâzim, ein offener Blick
in die Zukunft, lacht lauthals, dann schließt er
die Augen.

Life. An example

A book with pictures and photos of Nâzim Hikmet[1]
Falls into my hands:

Nâzim the revolutionary, unshaven, a coarse
Woollen scarf wrapped around his neck; Nâzim with
                                        Russian
Ballet teachers (is he learning how to change his step
Through history?); Nâzim as a child; Nâzim as a
Young naval cadet on the Red Islands; Nâzim in a martial
Mood in Anatolia; Nâzim
Staying abroad with friends, travelling
Peacefully, fleeing from Kemal; Nâzim
Lapping up the sun in prison in Hopa,
In Bursa, in Istanbul, Çankiri, and again in
Bursa; Nâzim on a hunger strike, Nâzim
Breaks the bread of his freedom
With Paul Robeson, Julius Fučik and Pablo Neruda
(they are all long-since dead); Nâzim
Fleeing across the Black
Sea, in Moscow, Berlin, in
Sofia and Peking, in Poland
Suspecting nothing, in Czechoslovakia and in Hungary,
                                        in France;
Nâzim with a broken heart at death's door
Rewriting the book of hours in Prague, experiencing his
First evening in Rome, inquiring mysteriously about
Paris, reporting from Havana, enjoying the disadvantages
Of exile, describing revolutionaries
As romantics (what would Nâzim have done
In a real revolution?); Nâzim shaving
In front of the mirror, Nâzim enjoying nature, falling in love
At the age of sixty, Nâzim cooking, being serious,
Reading the newspaper, Nâzim a candid look
At the future, laughing aloud, then closing
His eyes.

1980

[1]Nâzim Hikmet (1902–1963): Turkish revolutionary poet and
dramatist (transl. note).

Quer durch dies Haus

führt eine Grenze auf der einen Seite die Liebe
auf der anderen Seite der Tod abwechselnd
werden die begriffe verwechselt bis die Sprache
verstummt bis ein Herz in tausend gläserne
Augen zerspringt dann kommen die Maulwürfe
Lurche um den Menschen endlich Beine zu machen
zum aufrechten Gang zu verhelfen dann sollen
sie gehen dorthin woher sie gekommen sind und
dort eine bessere Welt bauen als diese die
von Gott stammt oder vom Kaiser von China oder
vom real existierenden Kapital sie sollen viel
Geld verdienen und gleich sein untereinander
die Haare mögen ihnen ausfallen auf dem Weg in
die Zukunft dann wird man endlich sehen daß es
darunter gar keine Köpfe gibt als höchstens
zur Tarnung jenes Loches in dem der eiserne
Vogel sitzt den man zu deutsch Seele nennt

Right through this house

There runs a border line. On one side love,
On the other side death, the concepts
Getting mixed up, each in turn, until language
Becomes mute, until the heart shatters
Into a thousand glass eyes. Then come the moles,
Amphibians, to get the human beings moving at last,
Help them walk on their own hind legs. May they
Set off to wherever they came from
And build a better world there than this one
Created by God or the Emperor of China or
Capital in its present form. May they
Make a lot of money and live in equality.
May their hair fall out on their road to
The future when at last it becomes clear
That there are no heads under it at all, except perhaps
To camouflage the hole in which the iron
Bird sits which in German we call the soul.

Abschied

Besoffen sterben, wie
der antike Dichter Nedim.
In klassischem Versmaß, kopfüber
ins Goldene Horn. Dort, zwischen Autowracks
und vergifteten Fischen, dort ist
er gestorben, nichts
als ein Kommentar
zur Geschichte.

Mauer, Nagel, Bild
(Für C.M.)

Mein Gedicht ist ein Nagel
in einer Mauer.

Daran hängt mein Gedicht,
ein Bild von der Mauer
mit einem Nagel darin.

Departure

To die drunk like
The ancient poet Nedim.[1]
In classical metre, headfirst
Into the Golden Horn. There, among the car wrecks
And poisoned fish, there
He died, no more
Than an exegesis
Of history.

Wall, nail, picture
(for C.M.)

My poem is a nail
In a wall.

On it hangs my poem,
A picture of the wall
With a nail in it.

[1]Nedim (1681–1730); prominent Turkish poet of the 'Tulip Age' who
died during the Patrona uprising in 1730 (transl. note.)

William Totok

(1951–)

Totok was born on 21 April 1951 in Comloşu Mare (Großkomlosch) in Banat and studied German and Romance philology in Timişoara (Temeswar). He was a member of the literary circle 'Aktionsgruppe Banat' (Banat Action Group) during the liberal period of the early seventies. In 1975–1976 he spent eight months under political arrest and was unable to publish for several years, working among other things in a brickyard. From 1979 to 1982 he taught German in Tomnatic (Triebswetter) and worked thereafter for the Timişoara German-language newspaper 'Neue Banater Zeitung'. In 1985 he was fired for political reasons and emigrated to West Berlin in 1987.

Arbeiter in der Ziegelei

die hände voll lärm
und aus der presse tropft viereckig-weicher ton
wie perlen
die finger greifen in die kühle masse
vor arbeitswut heult der motor

die esse fächert in den himmel schwarzen rauch
vermischt mit schweiß
und tränend schauen augen
der sonne nach
die in einem wolkentümpel badet

zurück ins preßhaus fallen strahlen
durch lücken in der alten wand

verschwitzt greift wieder nur ein menschenarm
die ziegel auf vom allerschnellsten band

Workers at the brickyard

Hands full of noise
And out of the press soft quadrangular clay drips
Like pearls.
Fingers grab at the cool substance,
The engine howling passionately.

The chimney-stack fans black smoke mixed with sweat
Into the sky
And tearful eyes
Gaze towards the sun
Bathing in a pool of clouds.

Rays filter back into the press house
Through gaps in the old wall.

Only a sweaty human arm grabs bricks
Again off the swift conveyor-belt.

Anna Espresso, Váci-utca,
Budapest, den 27. Juli 1979

es ist windig
und die Zeit sitzt auf den weißen Stühlen
des Lokals
ich schlürfe bitteren Kaffee
ein Alter gesellt sich zu mir
in seinen Augen blinkt das Jahrhundert
verwundert hört er mir zu
was ich da erzähle
über das Land aus welchem ich komme

gestern kaufte ich mir Ossip Mandelstams Gedichte
und ich schilderte dem Alten das Leben des Dichters
er fragt wie ich lebe
was ich schreibe und wieviel ich verdiene
es gibt Dinge die Sie nicht begreifen können
sage ich abschließend

schließlich gehen wir essen
egalwas sage ich
mein Geld geht mir langsam aus

Anna Espresso, Váci St., Budapest, 27 July 1979

It's windy out
And time reclines on the white chairs
Of the café
I sip my bitter coffee
An old man joins me
The whole century flashing in his eyes
He listens in surprise
To what I have to say
About the country I come from

Yesterday I bought Osip Mandel'shtam's poems
And told the old man about the poet's life
He asks what I live on
What I write about and how much I earn
There are things you cannot understand
I finally say

Then we go for something to eat
Anything'll do I say
My money's beginning to run out

Abschied

Ich zerschneide den Winter in kleine Stücke;
nur im Zugabteil ists warm.
Deine Hand winkt.
Die Schienen blinken matt, kurz
vor dem Abschied schreit die Lokomotive laut auf.
Deine Hand erstarrt.
Ich trage den Geruch deiner Haut in meiner Tasche.
Es wird so ruhig neben mir.
Deine Scham, deine Brüste – meine Heimat
gleitet davon im zergehenden Schnee.
Deine Hand hängt bewegungslos im Fenster.
Dein Bild geht neben mir.
Ich zerschneide es in kleine Stücke;
nur in meinem Zimmer ists warm.
Deine Hand winkt wie die wackligen Zeiger meiner Uhr.

Departure

I cut winter up into little pieces;
Only in the train compartment is it warm.
Your hand waves.
The tracks gleam faintly, just
Before departure the locomotive shrieks.
Your hand freezes.
I carry the fragrance of your skin in my pocket.
It's become so quiet beside me.
Your womb, your breasts – my homeland
Slips away in the melting snow.
Your hand hangs motionless in the window.
Your image walks beside me.
I cut it up into little pieces;
Only in my room is it warm.
You wave like the wobbly hands of my clock.

Jahreszeiten

Es ist so weit,
hinter deinen Augen
rasseln die Wärter mit den Schlüsseln.
Es gibt nichts mehr zu verpassen.
Den Bäumen brechen die Äste
unter dem Schnee,
in den Scheunen ists ruhig.
Deine Augen
sind jetzt zwei ausgebrannte Glühbirnen.

Petroleum fließt in den Sand.

Seasons

The time has come,
The guards are rattling their keys
Behind your back.
There's nothing else to miss.
The branches of the trees are cracking
Under the snow,
It's quiet in the barns.
Your eyes
Are now two burnt-out lightbulbs.

Petroleum seeps into the sand.

Gewöhnlicher Tag

dein Gesicht
ist im Nebel versteckt

ein ahnungsloser Beamter
fährt vorbei

nichts wirkt verdächtig
außer deinem unmerklichen Zwinkern

Die Fahne

Ich halt sie noch
Die Fahne und denk'
Sie nützt mir
Wenns mich friert

Normal day

Your face
Is hidden in the fog

Some unsuspecting official
Drives by

Nothing looks suspicious
But your subtle blink

The flag

I'm still holding
The flag and think
It might come in handy
If I freeze.

Rolf Bossert

(1952–1986)

He was born in the industrial town of
Reşiţa (Reschitza) in the Banat moun-
tains on 16 December 1952. He studied
German and English in Bucharest and
taught German for four years in Buşteni.
He then returned to Bucharest, working
for the 'Friedrich Schiller' German cul-
tural centre and from 1981 on for Meri-
diane and Kriterion publishing com-
panies. In 1984 he applied for emigra-
tion, the result of which was that he
lost his job, was refused authorization
to publish and disappeared as a public
figure. In the same period, he had
several unpleasant encounters with the
Romanian secret service shortly before
he was able to leave the country with
his wife and two sons in December
1985. Bossert committed suicide in
Frankfurt on 17 February 1986, leaving
behind two thin volumes of verse
'Siebensachen' 1979 and 'Neuntöter'
1984).

Das kurze Gedicht vom kleinen frierenden Vogel

Mich friert,
sagte der kleine Vogel
und installierte sein Nest
unter der schützenden Hülle
einer Vogelscheuche.

Short poem on a little freezing bird

I'm freezing,
Said the little bird
And installed its nest
Under the protective garments
Of a scarecrow.

Künstler Kritiker & Krautsalat

sehen Sie meine damen und herren das ist
mein kleiner finger
so dünn daß Sie ihn kaum bemerken werden
ringfinger folgt
der eiserne ring zeugt von meiner ehelichen verbindung
mit ich weiß nicht wem
    die nächsten zwei
    — mittelfinger und zeigefinger —
    ständig erhoben
    mal eng aneinander mal zum V gespreizt
ich weiß nicht
soll mein daumen nach unten oder nach oben zeigen
    aber
mit allen fünf fingern greife ich
in die salatschüssel
denn mir schmeckt krautsalat

Artists, critics & cabbage salad

You see, ladies and gentlemen, this is
My little finger
So thin you hardly notice it
Next is my ring finger
The iron ring is proof of my marital ties
With someone or other
    the next two
    — the middle and index fingers —
    are always up in the air
    sometimes together sometimes in a V
I don't know
Whether my thumb should be pointing up or down
    but
With all five fingers I dig
Into the salad-bowl
Because I love cabbage salad

Goldne Zeiten der Fabel

löwe und maus
vertieft im fachgespräch:
was leichter zu durchbeißen sei?

stricke sagte die maus
kehlen sagte der löwe

wie dem auch sei:
den erhängten
kriegten sie runter vom baum

(das war eine große tat:
der tote stinkt nicht mehr gen himmel
sondern in unserer näh)

Golden age of fables

Lion and mouse
Engrossed in a discussion:
Which is easier to bite through?

Ropes said the mouse,
Necks said the lion.

At any rate
They got the hanged man
Down off the tree

(it was a feat:
The deadman no longer reeks to the heavens,
But among us).

Aus meinem Leben

24. september 1977
ich bin verheiratet und habe zwei kinder meine
frau lehrt deutsch als fremdsprache ich auch wir
bewohnen zwei zimmer einer dreizimmerwoh-
nung das kleine zimmer ist sieben komma sie-
benundachtzig quadratmeter groß das große zim-
mer ist neun komma achtundachtzig quadrat-
meter groß das größte zimmer der wohnung ist
vierzehn komma neunundsechzig quadratmeter
groß wir wohnen nicht darin es ist abgesperrt
meist steht es leer aber im winter wohnt ein
altes ehepaar in dem zimmer so sparen die leute
holz bei sich zu hause auf dem dorf oft kommen
an wochenenden unbekannte familien mit kin-
dern die höhenluft tut den kleinen gut die drei-
zimmerwohnung liegt im schönen luftkurort
buşteni küche badezimmer und klo werden von
vielen personen benützt nur der balkon liegt
an der sonnenseite er gehört zum dritten zimmer
ich darf ihn nicht betreten
ich habe ans wohnungsamt geschrieben
an den volksrat
an die zeitung
ich habe bei vielen genossen vorgesprochen
nun schreibe ich ein gedicht
ich habe unbegrenztes vertrauen in die macht
der poesie

21. dezember 1977
dieser text ist unveröffentlicht gestern bekamen
die alten zwei zimmer in einer villa wir bekamen
den schlüssel zum dritten zimmer womit bewie-
sen ist daß auch unveröffentlichte gedichte die
realität aus der sie schöpfen verändern können
ich werde noch gedichte schreiben

About my life

24 September 1977
I'm married and have two children my wife
Teaches German as a foreign language so do I we
Live in two rooms of a three-room apartment
The little room is seven point eighty-seven
Square metres the big room is nine
Point eighty-eight square metres
The biggest room in the apartment is
Fourteen point sixty-nine square metres
We don't use it it's locked and is
Empty most of the time but in the winter
An elderly couple uses it to save on
Firewood at home in their village families we don't know
often come up on weekends with their children
The mountain air's good for the kids the three-room
Apartment is situated in the beautiful mountain resort
Of Buşteni kitchen bathroom and toilet are shared by
A lot of people only the balcony
Faces south it belongs to the third room
I'm not allowed to use it
I've written to the housing authorities
To the people's council
To the newspaper
I've called on quite a number of officials
Now I'm writing a poem
I have infinite confidence in the power
Of poetry

21 December 1977
This text hasn't been published yesterday the
Elderly couple got two rooms in a mansion
We got the key to the third room which goes
To prove that even unpublished poems can change
The reality from which they draw their inspiration
I intend to write more poems

Jahreszeit

Hinaus in den fahlen Tag
stiegen wir, birkenwärts
Vorbei an Höfen
aus Rauch: Krematorien
für die Wimpern des Herbstes.

Nackte, goldene Augen
blickten uns an.

Am Abend
schläft deine Hand
neben mir.

Season

Out into the pale day
We went, beechward.
Past yards
Full of smoke: crematoria
For autumn's eyelashes.

Naked, golden eyes
Were watching us.

At night
Your hand sleeps
Next to me.

Nachtschattenriß

Die stehn vor der Tür, mit
Hammer und Chrysanthemen:
keine Gäste, Arbeiter nicht.
Das sind keine Russen, die
stieben nicht durch die Zacken
ewig komplementärer Gedanken.
Die lieben die Schönheit
den Stilbruch. Doch sinds nicht
die ledernen Engel des Herrn.
Die wolln deine Haut, meine Wörter.

Zuversicht

Das Blei ist träge,
noch steckt die Kugel im Lauf.
So haben wir Zeit.

Nightshade rift

They're standing outside the door
With hammers and chrysanthemums:
Not guests, not workers.
They're not the Russians,
They don't fly through the prongs
Of eternally complementary thoughts.
They love beauty,
Incongruities of style. But they're
Not the leather angels of the Lord.
They want your skin, my words.

Confidence[1]

The lead is sluggish.
Bullet still in the barrel.
And so we have time.

[1]The text is written in the form of a Japanese Haiku (transl. note).

Richard Wagner

(1952—)

Wagner was born in Lovrin (Lowrin) in Banat on 10 April 1952. He studied German in Timişoara (Temeswar) where he took part in the liberal literary movement 'Aktionsgruppe Banat' (Banat Action Group). From 1975 to 1978 he taught in Hunedoara and from 1979 to 1984 worked as a journalist for the Braşov (Kronstadt) weekly newspaper 'Karpaten Rundschau'. In March 1987 he emigrated to West Berlin. Wagner is author of six volumes of verse as well as prose and children's literature. He is married to prose writer Herta Müller.

Dialektik

wir haben die verhältnisse erkannt
wir haben beschlossen sie zu verändern

wir haben sie verändert

dann kamen andere
die haben die veränderten verhältnisse
erkannt und haben beschlossen
sie zu verändern

sie haben die veränderten verhältnisse
verändert

dann kamen andere
die haben die veränderten veränderten
verhältnisse erkannt und haben
beschlossen sie zu verändern

sie haben die veränderten veränderten
verhältnisse verändert

dann kamen andere

Dialectics

We grasped the situation
We resolved to change it

We changed it

Then others came along
They grasped the changed
Situation and resolved
To change it

They changed the changed
Situation

Then others came along
They grasped the changed changed
Situation and resolved
To change it

They changed the changed
Changed situation

Then others came along

Dichterworte

der mut sagte der dichter
der mut auch negative aspekte hob der dichter hervor
die für die gesellschaft keineswegs repräsentativ sind
räumte der dichter ein
sondern nur vereinzelt und spontan auftauchen
betonte der dichter
literarisch zu verarbeiten hauchte der dichter
wirkt sich zweifellos überaus positiv unterstrich
                                        der dichter
u. nicht umgekehrt fügte der dichter rasch hinzu
auf die entwicklung der gesellschaft aus
schloß der dichter

Words of the poet

Courage said the poet
Courage to deal in one's writing wheezed the poet
With certain negative aspects stressed the poet
Which are by no means representative of society as a
whole
Conceded the poet
But which simply arise sporadically and spontaneously
Emphasized the poet has without a doubt
An exceedingly positive effect underlined the poet
And not vice versa added the poet deftly
On the development of society
Concluded the poet

Die Kellnerin

Sie fliegt zwischen den Tischen hin
und her. Die Blicke eilen ihr nach,
die Hände winken sie ran. Sie

fliegt hin und her, balanciert das
Tablett, macht die Rechnung, zählt
das Geld, hat kein Kleingeld, bedankt

sich, lehnt am Tresen. Bringt den
Kaffee, wird nervös, diese Männer.
Alles fällt, alle Worte falln von ihr

ab. Kalt geht sie zwischen uns hin
und her. Ihre Stimme ist schneidend.
Danke, sagt sie. Vielen Dank. Dann

geht sie mit dem leeren Tablett zum
Tresen hin und jetzt. Ja, jetzt
macht sie diese Geste von früher,

jene Geste vom Land, das hat sie
noch nicht verlernt. Draußen steh
ich, seh sie noch immer vor mir.

The waitress

She flits back and forth
Among the tables. Eyes pursuing her,
Hands calling her attention. She

Flits back and forth, steadies
Her tray, writes the bills, counts
Her money, has no change, says

Thanks, leans on the counter. Brings
Coffee, gets jittery, these guys.
Everything falls, all the words glance

Off her. Indifferently she flits by us,
Back and forth. Her voice is shrill.
Thanks, she says, thanks very much. Then

She returns to the counter,
With her empty tray, and now look,
Now she's doing it, that old gesture,

That country gesture
She hasn't forgotten yet. I stand outside
And can still see her in front of me.

Frage an Mandelstam

ossip
        bruder
                wir sind öl im getriebe
ach wären wir doch öl auf feuer
                        aber wir sind
                                öl im getriebe
        ossip bruder
                gehen wir
                        funktioniert's schlechter
aber's funktioniert
                bruder
                        was soll'n
        wir tun

Question for Mandel'shtam[1]

Osip
    Brother
        We are oil in the works
Oh, if only we were oil on the fire
           But we are
               Oil in the works
    Osip brother
        When we move
           It works worse
But it works
    Brother
        What else can
We do

---

[1]Osip Mandel'shtam (1891–1938); Russian poet (transl. note).

Lied

die arbeit schlief
die dichtung schlief
der frieden schlief
die zukunft schlief
das war als die schweizergarde
den putschversuch unternahm

die arbeit erwachte
die dichtung erwachte
der frieden erwachte
die zukunft erwachte
das war als die schweizergarde
den putschversuch unternahm

die arbeit machte sich
über den frieden her
die dichtung machte sich
über die zukunft her
das war als die schweizergarde
den putschversuch unternahm

die arbeit wurde friedlich
die dichtung wurde zukünftig
das war als die schweizergarde
den putschversuch unternahm

Song

Work slept
Verse slept
Peace slept
The future slept
That was
When the Swiss Guard
Attempted
A coup d'état

Work awoke
Verse awoke
Peace awoke
The future awoke
That was
When the Swiss Guard
Attempted
A coup d'état

Work attacked
Peace
Verse attacked
The future
That was
When the Swiss Guard
Attempted
A coup d'état

Work became peaceful
Verse became futuristic
That was
When the Swiss Guard
Attempted
A coup d'état

Mit dem Maler Lauterbach

Sie kommen,
immer noch ohne Haussuchungsbefehl.
Sie nehmen Bilder mit,
immer noch Bilder.
Und die Nachbarn sind wütend,
immer noch,
weil sie mit den Bildern
die Wände im Treppenhaus
beschädigen.

Der brennende Tisch
(Nach einer Postkarte)

Am brennenden Tisch
saß ich
und schrieb.
Was ich schrieb,
hielt das Brennen
nicht auf.
Was brannte,
hinderte mich
am Schreiben
nicht.

With the painter Lauterbach

They still keep coming
Without a search warrant.
They take the pictures,
Still keep taking the pictures
And the neighbours are still
Furious
Because transporting the pictures,
They mark
The walls in the stairwell.

The burning table
(from a postcard)

I sat
At the burning table
And wrote.
What I wrote
Didn't stop
The burning.
What burned
Didn't stop
My writing.

Ich war ein Denkmal

ich war ein denkmal
an einem lauen morgen kletterte
ich von meinem sockel herab
wollte dem mann
der mich täglich abzustauben hatte
entgegen kommen

die leiter noch auf dem rücken
schaute der mich freundlich an
lächelte gekonnt
und drückte mir den lappen
in die hand

I was a statue

I was a statue.
One balmy morning
I climbed down off my pedestal
To meet the man
Who has to dust me off
Every day.

Carrying a ladder on his back
He gave me a friendly look,
An accomplished smile,
And handed me
His cloth.

Ernest Wichner

(1952—)

Wichner was born in Frumoşliu (Guttenbrunn) in Banat in 1952. He studied German and Political Science in Timişoara (Temeswar) and West Berlin. In 1975, he emigrated to the Federal Republic of Germany and has been living in West Berlin since 1976. He is the author of poetry, prose, essays, translations and criticism.

Losung

bannmeilenweit Glück und wir
bunte Seifenblasen
über behelmten Köpfen
der Nacht

Slogan

All through the government quarter, happiness and us
Colourful soap bubbles
Over the helmeted heads
Of the night

Trakl im Exil

aus dem kalifornischen Exil,
bekannt ist, daß Trakl die
Einladungen Brechts mit „Sebastian

schläft" beschriftet zurückge-
wiesen hat, schreibt der 54jährige
an seine 49jährige Schwester

Grete: „ . . . es ist dahin; die Mes-
singträume abgespult, aufgegeben,
was Sinn zu haben schien. Groß

hängt, was Traum gewesen, greifbar:
die Wörter, Grete, die Wörter . . .
ich hab sie gesehen, wie sie die

Stiege hoch kamen und mit aller
Gewalt zu mir rein wollten; reden,
sagten sie, reden wollten sie

mit mir. Ich aber, die Kette vor
der Tür, verharrte still nach in-
nen bangend, war einfach nicht da."

Trakl in exile[1]

We know that Trakl
Rejected Brecht's invitations
From his Californian exile,

Inscribing on them 'Sebastian
Is asleep', the 54-year-old wrote
To his 49-year-old sister

Grete: ' . . . it's all over, the brass dreams
Unwound, abandoned
All that seemed to be meaningful.

What once was dreams hangs large, tangible:
The words, Grete, the words . . .
I saw them as they came

Up the stairs and tried
To force their way in; to talk,
They said, they just wanted to talk

To me. But I, with a chain
On the door, remained inside
In silent anguish, was simply not there.'

[1]Georg Trakl (1887–1914); Austrian poet (transl. note).

Horst Samson

(1954—)

Born on 4 June 1954 in the village of Salcîmi in the Baragan steppe of south-eastern Romania where his family had been deported, Samson studied at the teacher training college in Sibiu (Hermannstadt) and at the Faculty of Journalism of the Academy of Social Sciences in Bucharest. He worked from 1974 to 1977 as a teacher, from 1977 to 1984 on the editorial staff of the 'Neue Banater Zeitung' in Timişoara (Temeswar) and from 1984 to 1987 for the influential literary periodical 'Neue Literatur' in Bucharest. On 6 March 1987 he emigrated to the Federal Republic of Germany and now lives in Leonberg near Stuttgart. Samson is the author of four volumes of poetry published in Romania as well as of short stories and criticism.

Reise nach Paris

pont neuf comédie française
père-lachaise champs élysées

ich bin doch da
angekommen ohne abzufahren

seht ihr mich nicht vom gehsteig aus
wie ich mit meinem schreibtisch
durch paris rase

salut
ruft der invalidendom mir zu

Trip to Paris

Pont Neuf Comédie Française
Père Lachaise Champs Elysées

I'm here
Arrived without having left

Can't you see me from the sidewalk
Speeding through Paris
With my desk

Salut
The Dôme des Invalides calls out to me.

Morgen

der schlüssel dreht sich im schloß
dumpf schlägt die tür gegen die wand
dumpf schlägt sie zu
ich höre wie du die milchflaschen
auf den küchentisch stellst
(sie klirren leise wie eiswürfel)
dann kommst du herein zu mir
da bin ich sagst du
und legst einen stapel zeitungen auf den tisch

Morning

The key turns in the lock
The door bumps against the wall
It closes with a thud
I hear you putting the milk bottles
On the kitchen table
(they clink gently like ice-cubes)
Then you come into my room
I'm back you say
And lay a stack of newspapers on the table.

Pünktlicher Lebenslauf
(nachbar hans zum 60.)

nachts setzt sich nachbar hans
den stahlhelm auf
steckt sich ein gebetbuch
in die brusttasche
und fährt mit einem schwarzen nsu
durch ein minenfeld bei narwa
in richtung leningrad

morgens um fünf
ist er wieder da

Punctual curriculum vitae
(For my neighbour Hans on his 60th birthday)

At night my neighbour Hans
Puts his steel helmet on
Sticks a prayer book
In his breast pocket
And drives a black NSU
Through a minefield near Narva
On towards Leningrad

At five in the morning
He's back

Schneegedicht für Edda

der raum für uns
ist so eng
    zwischen den schlagzeilen

so bald wird sich da nichts ändern

meine texte könnte ich ins feuer werfen
danach ein geständnis machen und aufgeben
    eine wand würde fallen

doch wüßte ich nachher noch wer ich bin

vor unserer tür liegen schneeberge
viele winzige lichter
    ich weiß daß jeden tag einige davon erlöschen

der winter ist kalt und lang

Snow poem for Edda

The room for us
Between the headlines
   Is so constricting

Nothing is going to change very fast

I could throw my texts into the fire
Then make a confession and give up
   A wall would crumble

And afterwards I would still know who I am

In front of our door are mounds of snow
A lot of tiny lights
   I know that some go out every day

Winter is cold and long

Schässburger Dichtertreffen
(Gaststätte „Vlad Dracul")

die steine rücken zusammen
die mauern wachsen in den nachmittag

im geschichtebuch schreien
die gepfählten türken

der blutige graf aus den karpaten
er lebt

der burgberg die spitzen türme reglos
im wind
das stehengebliebene wort

nur wenige drehen sich noch
in den kaffeeschalen hin und her

ab und zu hebt ein dichter den kopf
aus dem bierschaum

auf den sträßen
baumeln die besiegten

Meeting of poets in Sighişoara
('Vlad Dracul' Restaurant)

The stones convene
The walls grow into the afternoon

Impaled Turks
Scream in the annals of history

The bloodthirsty Carpathian count
Lives

The hilltop castles the pointed roofs motionless
In the wind
The word which has come to a halt

A few still sway
Back and forth in the coffee cups

Now and then a poet raises his head
Out of the beer suds

In the streets
The vanquished dangle

Verinselung
(für Franz Hodjak)

weniger geworden
schnappen wir nach luft
nach mehr luft
in langen todbringenden nächten
sitzen wir am steinernen tisch
trinken den letzten bohnenkaffee
den wir aufgehoben haben
für schwarze zeiten

und ich sage dir das gedicht
und du sagst ihm das gedicht
und er sagt mir das gedicht
das ich dir dann weitersage

gegen morgen springen wir
in die weinflaschen
und gehen unter

Isolation
(for Franz Hodjak)

Fewer now
We gasp for air
For more air
In long death-bearing nights
We sit around the stone table
Drinking the last coffee
We were saving
For a rainy day

And I tell you the poem
And you tell him the poem
And he tells me the poem
Which I then tell you

At daybreak we leap
Into the wine bottles
And drown

Urlaub im Zimmer

wir baden in unserer leeren brieftasche
halten medusen gegen das untergehende licht
der stehlampe

lachen und singen klatschen und tanzen
auf dem weißen leintuch
werfen salz wie meersand in die luft

leise küsse ich
ihre braune haut

im radio rauscht das meer
schlägt hohe wellen

die sonne scheint
viereckig

und pepsi gibts
auf dem bildschirm in rauhen mengen

mit verdrehten augen
laufen wir glücklich über den strand
in den spitzen schrei einer möwe

Holidays at home

We go for a swim in our empty wallet
Hold jellyfish up against the twilight
Of the lamp

Laugh and sing, clap and dance
On the white linen tablecloth
Throw salt into the air like sand at the beach

Gently I kiss
Her brown skin

The sea roars on the radio
Its mighty waves breaking

The sun looks
Rectangular

And there's lots of Pepsi
On the screen

With crazy eyes
We sprint joyfully down the beach
Into the shrill cry of a seagull

Wintermorgen
(für R.W.)

motto
das hat man davon
die leute lieben zu laut

um halbfünf morgens
knirscht der schnee
unter den schuhsohlen
wir sind wach
warten auf milch
und der frost schüttelt uns
neben mir
wünscht sich jemand
eine milchwolke
in den kühlschrank
plötzlich wünschen sich
zweihundert leute
milchwolken
in den kühlschrank

dort drüben sind die fenster
noch dunkel
sagt jemand
denen gehts gut
die schlafen

wie gut gehts denen
die schlafen

Winter morning
(for R.W.)

Motto:
There you have it!
People love too loudly

At four thirty in the morning
The snow crunches
Under the soles of our shoes
We are awake
Waiting for milk
And shiver in the frost
Next to me
Someone wishes
He had a milk cloud
In his fridge
All of a sudden
Two hundred people wish
They had milk clouds
In their fridges

On the other side the windows
Are still dark
Someone says
They're lucky
They're sleeping

How lucky they are
They're sleeping

Wintergedicht für Sarah Kirsch

nordwind bläst
aus den büchern herüber

schwer liegt der winter
über dem land

die leute sind ruhig und eingeschlossen
im pelzmantel

die krähen sitzen
im hals

der schnee denke ich
ist ein weißes märchen
das lügt

Winter poem for Sarah Kirsch[1]

North wind blows
Over to us out of books

Winter lies heavy
On the land

People are quiet and bundled up
In fur coats

Crows perch
In throats

Snow I think
Is a white fairy tale
That lies

[1]Sarah Kirsch (1935—): German poet (transl. note).

Federico

die welt
einsam und fern

der morgen eine ahnung
unter den hufen des lichts

ein dunkles pferd am zügel
kommt Federico durch den riß in der wand
gebirgsgras in den augenhöhlen
ein brennendes gedicht im mund
zeigt mir seine wunde die weitoffene gitarre

über meine gesammelt weggeschleppten texte
bücher und tonbänder hinweg
folge ich ihm
in den finsteren blick des gewehrlaufs

Federico

The world
Lonely and distant

The morning an inkling
Under hooves of light

At the reins of a dark horse
Federico comes in through the crack in the wall
Mountain grass in the sockets of his eyes
A fiery poem in his mouth
And shows me his wound the gaping guitar

With my texts, books and tapes
All spirited off
I follow him
Into the dark path of the gun barrel

Nachbemerkung zu meiner Geburt

unter der fleckigen sonne
der baragansteppe
wurde ich geboren
neben einer distel
oder an einem anderen tag

damals sah ich gar nichts

so dunkel und so ungenau
war die geschichte
meiner geburt

Subsequent remark about my birth

Under the motley sun
Of the Baragan steppe
I was born
Beside a thistle
Or on another day

I saw nothing at the time

So obscure and imprecise
Was the story
Of my birth

Carmen Puchianu

(1956—)

Puchianu was born on 27 November 1956. After secondary school graduation in Braşov (Kronstadt), she studied English and German in Bucharest from 1975 to 1979. She now teaches at the Johannes Honterus secondary school in Braşov.

Postkarte an Frank O'Hara

Von Glaskugeln verzerrt
hängen fremde Hände mir ins Gesicht.
Die Postkarte an Frank
schreibe ich nicht.
Ich malte sie viel eher
als Stilleben
mit Apfel und Schlange
auf der Waage im Gleichgewicht.

Zeitlos

Genehmigt mir die stille
Stunde mitternächtlichen
Herbstes,
das rostige Rauschen
zeitloser Schritte im gelblichen Gras.

Unvermeidlich
steht uns allen Schnee bevor.

Postcard for Frank O'Hara

Distorted by crystal balls
Strange hands hang in my face.
I am not going to write
The postcard to Frank.
I'll paint it instead
As a still life
With an apple and a snake
Balanced on the scales.

Timeless

Grant me the quiet
Hour of a midnight
Autumn,
The rusty rustle
Of timeless steps in the fallow grass.

Inevitably
Snow lies ahead for us all.

Juliana Modoi

(1962–)

Juliana Modoi was born on 8 August 1962 in Braşov (Kronstadt) and studied German in Bucharest from 1981 to 1986. Her first verse appeared in the Braşov weekly periodical 'Karpatenrundschau' in 1972. She is not only a poet but also an expert in the game of chess.

Dorfabend

Der Schimmer des Abends
zieht an den Hufen der Büffel
langsam durch die Gassen;
mit federleichter Hand
deutet ein Schatten
auf unser Haus.
Die Umrisse
morgiger Gäste
zeichnet er
mit dem Finger
in die Luft.

Der Trost einer Mutter

Wenn es dunkelt,
darf ich nicht weinen,
denn in meinem Innern
hört mich dein Kind.

Village evening

The pale light of evening
Saunters through the streets
On buffalo hooves;
With a hand light as a feather
A shadow
Points at our house.
With a finger
In the air
It draws
The counters
Of tomorrow's guests.

A mother's consolation

I am not allowed to weep
When it gets dark
For your child is listening
Within me.

Bibliography

BERWANGER, NIKOLAUS
Spätes Bekenntnis. Lyrische Texte (Kriterion. Bucharest 1979)
Schneewittchen öffne deine Augen. Lyrische Texte (Facla. Timişoara 1980)
An meine ungeborenen Enkel. Lyrische Texte (Facla. Timişoara 1983)
Offene Milieuschilderung. Lyrische Texte (Olms. Hildesheim 1985)
In Liebe und in Haß. Der grofe Schaubenausverkauf und andere Texte
(Olms. Hildesheim 1987)
BOSSERT, ROLF
Siebensachsen. Gedichte (Kriterion. Bucharest 1979)
Neuntöter. Gedichte (Dacia. Cluj-Napoca 1984)
Auf der Milchstraße wieder kein Licht. Gedichte (Rotbuch. West Berlin
1986)
HOCKL, HANS WOLFRAM ET AL.
Heimatbuch der Donauschwaben (Munich 1959)
HODJAK, FRANZ
Spielräume. Gedichte & Einfälle (Kriterion. Bucharest 1974)
Offene Briefe. Gedichte (Kriterion. Bucharest 1976)
Mit Polly Knall spricht man über selbstverständliche Dinge als wären
sie selbstverständlich. Gedichte (Kriterion. Bucharest 1979)
Flieder im Ohr. Gedichte (Kriterion. Bucharest 1983)
Sehnsucht nach Feigenschnaps. Ausgewёhlte Gedichte (Aufbau. East
Berlin 1988)
LATZINA, ANEMONE
Was man heute so dichten kann. Gedichte (Kriterion. Bucharest 1971)
Lichtkaskaden. Ein Jubiläumsanthologie (23. August 1944 – 23. August
1984) (Kriterion. Bucharest 1984)
LIPPET, JOHANN
So wars im Mai so ist es. Gedichte (Kriterion. Bucharest 1984)
MARMONT, ROLF FRIEDER
Fünfte Jahreszeit. Gedichte (Dacia. Cluj-Napoca 1974)
MODOI, JULIANA
Dorfabend. Der Zweite Horizont (Dacia, Cluj 1988)
Der Trost einer Mutter. Der Zweite Horizont (Dacia, Cluj 1988)
MOTZAN, PETER
Die rumäniendeutsche Lyrik nach 1944 (Dacia. Cluj-Napoca 1980)
MOTZAN, PETER (ED.)
Vorläufige Protokolle. Anthologie junger rumäniendeutscher Lyrik
(Dacia. Cluj-Napoca 1976)
Der Herbst stöbert in den Blättern. Deutschsprachige Lyrik aus
Rumänien (Volk und Welt. East Berlin 1984)
PASTIOR, OSKAR
Gedichtgedichte (Heyne. Munich 1982)
Höricht (Ramm. Spenge 1979)
PUCHIANU, CARMEN
Postkarte an Frank O'Hara. Der Zweite Horizont (Dacia, Cluj 1988)
Zeitlos. Der Zweite Horizont (Dacia, Cluj 1988)
SAMSON, HORST
Tiefflug. Gedichte (Dacia. Cluj-Napoca 1981)
Reibefläche. Gedichte (Kriterion. Bucharest 1982)
Lebraum (Dacia. Cluj-Napoca 1985)
SCHERER, ANTON
Die nicht sterben wollten. Donauschwäbische Literatur von Lenau

bis zur Gegenwart (Freilassing 1959)
Einführung in die Geschichte der donauschwäbischen Literatur (Graz 1960)
Donauschwäbische Bibliographie 1935–1955 (Verlag des Südostdeutschen Kulturwerks. Munich 1966)
Südosteuropa-Dissertationen 1918–1960 (Böhlau. Graz, Vienna, Cologne 1968)
Die Literatur der Donauschwaben als Mittlerin zwischen Völkern und Kulturen (Graz 1972)
Donauschwäbische Bibliographie 1955–1965 (Verlag des Südostdeutschen Kulturwerks. Munich (1974)

SCHNEIDER, EDUARD (ED.)
Wortmeldungen. Eine Anthologie junger Lyrik aus dem Banat (Facla. Timişoara 1972)

SCHNEIDER, HELMUT
Das Banat. Eine abendländische Landschaft (Theiss. Stuttgart 1986)

SCHULLER, FRIEDER
Pass für Transsilvanien. Gedichte (Urheber Verlag. Bonn 1979)
Einladung zu einer Schüssel Palukes (Parnaß. Bonn 1980)

SCHWOB, ANTON
Beiträge zur deutschen Literatur in Rumänien seit 1918 (Verlag des Südostdeutschen Kulturwerks. Munich 1985)

SIENERTH, STEFAN (ED.)
Wintergrün. Anthologie siebenbürgisch-deutscher Lyrik aus der zweiten Hälfte des 19. Jahrhunderts. Auswahl, Vorwort und bio-bibliographischer Anhang (Dacia. Cluj-Napoca 1978)
Wahrheit vom Brot. Anthologie siebenbürgisch-deutscher Lyrik der Jahrhundertwende. Auswahl, Vorwort und bio-bibliographischer Anhang (Dacia. Cluj-Napoca 1980)
Ausklang. Anthologie siebenbürgisch-deutscher Lyrik der Zwischenkriegszeit. Auswahl, Vorwort und bio-bibliographischer Anhang (Dacia. Cluj-Napoca 1982)
Geschichte der siebenbürgisch-deutschen Literatur von den Anfängen bis zum Ausgang des 16. Jh. (Dacia. Cluj-Napoca 1984)

SÖLLNER, WERNER
Mitteilungen eines Privatmannes. Gedichte (Dacia. Cluj-Napoca 1978)
Eine Entwöhnung. Gedichte (Kriterion. Bucharest 1980)
Kopfland. Passagen. Gedichte (Suhrkamp. Frankfurt 1988)

STEPHANI, CLAUS
Ruf ins offene Land. Lyrische Texte (Kriterion. Bucharest 1975)
Draussen singt Dorkia. Lyrische Marginalien (Kriterion. Bucharest 1985)

STEPHANI, CLAUS (ED.)
Befragung heute. Junge deutsche Lyrik in Rumänien. Mit sechzehn Graphiken (Kriterion. Bucharest 1974)

STIEHLER, HEINRICH (ED.)
Nachrichten aus Rumänien. Rumäniendeutsche Literatur. Auslandsdeutsche Literatur der Gegenwart. Band 2 (Olms. Hildesheim, New York 1976)

TOTOK, WILLIAM
Die Vergesellschaftung der Gefühle. Gedichte (Kriterion. Bucharest 1980)
Freundliche Fremdheit. Gedichte (Facla. Timişoara 1984)

WAGNER, RICHARD
Klartext. Ein Gedichtbuch (Albatros. Bucharest 1973)
Die Invasion der Uhren. Gedichte (Kriterion. Bucharest 1977)
Hotel California 1. Gedichte (Kriterion. Bucharest 1980)
Hotel California 2. Gedichte (Kriterion. Bucharest 1981)

Gegenlicht. Gedichte (Facla. Timişoara 1983)
Das Auge des Feuilletons. Geschichten und Notizen (Dacia.
  Cluj-Napoca 1984)
WICHNER, ERNEST
  Steinsuppe, Gedichte (Suhrkamp. Frankfurt 1988)
WICHNER, ERNEST (ED.)
  Das Wohnen ist kein Ort. Texte und Zeichen aus Siebenbürgen, dem
  Banat und den Gegenden versuchter Ankunft. in: Die Horen,
  Zeitschrift für Literatur, Kunst und Kritik 147 (Hanover 1987)

Also from
Forest Books

ANTHOLOGY OF SORBIAN POETRY
FROM THE SIXTEENTH CENTURY
TO THE PRESENT DAY

The Sorbs or Wends are a Slavic minority living in
Germany. Despite the decimation of the First World
War and the stifling oppression of the 'Aryan' dic-
tatorship of the Third Reich, Sorbian literature has
flourished, making a substantial contribution to the
mosaic of European culture, a tiny but unique voice
in a great choir. The present anthology, richly illust-
rated by Silke Ulbricht, an introductory selection of
Sorbian verse from its beginnings in the sixteenth
century to the present day, is the first of its kind in
English.

ISBN 0948259 72 8   paper £6.95   96pp illustrated